OUT OF TIME?

JONATHAN NEWDICK

Out of time?

Published on the occasion of
the exhibition 'Out of time?'
at The Weald and Downland
Open-air Museum at
Singleton near Chichester
(www.wealddown.co.uk)
from June 30 to July 12,
2012.

Designed and published by
Jonathan Newdick in an
edition of 500 copies, typeset
in Monotype Bell 341 and
printed in England at
The Lavenham Press
(www.lavenhampress.com)

ISBN 978-0-9572404-0-7
www.jonathannewdick.co.uk

CONTENTS

ACKNOWLEDGEMENTS

No-one can undertake an exercise such as this without the kindness and hospitality of the landowners, tenant farmers, gamekeepers and others on whose land I have spent the best part of a couple of years. They are too many to mention individually and, if I were to, the list would somehow dilute their individual importance to my task on any one day. I thank them all. Among individuals, David Coke gave valuable help with his critical appraisal of my introduction. I am deeply grateful to Alexandra Harris who somehow found the time in her busy schedule to write the foreword. Her supportive e-mails seemed always to arrive at moments of doubt. Dr Annabelle Hughes gave assistance with the historical details noted in the postscript and I am indebted to Richard Pailthorpe and the staff at the Weald and Downland Open-air Museum for giving me the opportunity to hold the exhibition at a venue which could not have been more apposite.
Finally (and finally only by virtue of her Italian surname), my thanks go to Fulvia Zavan without whose unwavering support none of this would have happened.

COVER ILLUSTRATION

The illustration on the cover is a colour enhanced version of catalogue number 41 and includes the artist's notes which were used to form the text which accompanies the drawing. It is reproduced to the same size as the original. The texts are not always written on the drawing paper; often they are in a notebook or just on a scrap of paper. Where they are on the drawing they have usually been kept, though they will be covered by the mount and the frame of the finished picture.

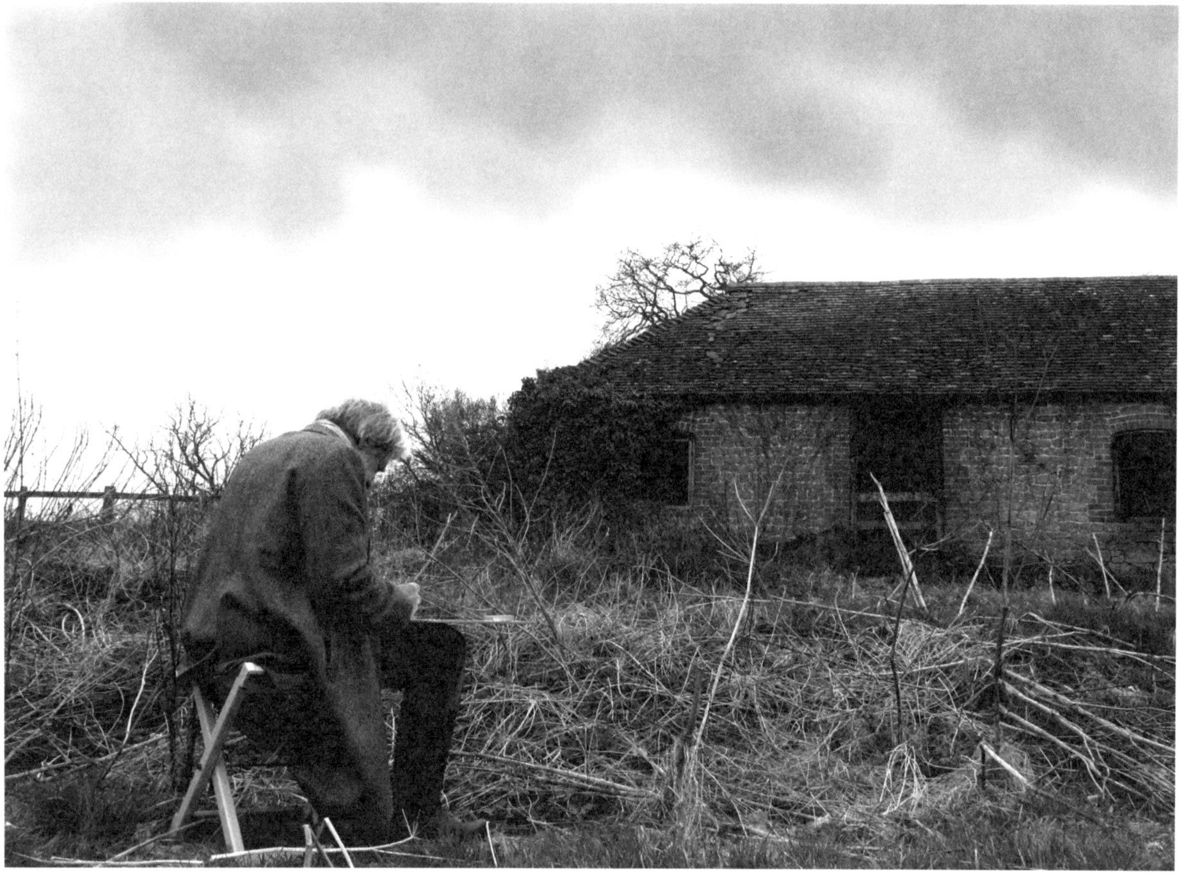

Jonathan Newdick at work on the drawing of abandoned farm buildings on the River Rother near Petworth. (Catalogue number 11). Photograph by Fulvia Zavan.

FOREWORD

Alexandra Harris, writer, critic, and lecturer in English at the University of Liverpool

I came to know Jonathan Newdick and his work only in 2011 but in that short time I have seen a great many of his drawings of buildings and landscape. Each is mesmerising; each is a surprise, a whole new prospect, a different way of thinking and looking.

Newdick has been drawing farm outbuildings in Sussex since the autumn of 2009, concentrating at first on the Leconfield Estate in Petworth, and then going a little further afield – rarely more than walking distance. Many of the buildings he chooses are in varying states of abandonment and collapse, left behind by the new scale and technologies of modern agriculture. A threshing barn, once the largest and most important building on a farm, is now surplus to requirements; a cart shed cannot accommodate a combine harvester. These structures were built with skill and pride and style, but what is their fate today? They cannot be conserved in any number, and rural England has no duty to be a museum of its past. One by one the barns will disappear. But look at them before they go, that is what Newdick asks: decide what is valuable, consider whether there are traces here of attitudes we may want in future to recover.

These drawings are very much in the spirit of the 'Recording Britain' project which flourished during World War Two. And they re-invigorate a topographical tradition which has run continuously through English art, from the exquisite draughtsmanship of Paul Sandby in the eighteenth century, through Samuel Palmer's lichened barns at Shoreham, to Eric Ravilious's leaning fence posts in the 1930s. Like his predecessors, Newdick is a recorder of places on the verge of change, but he is not only a recorder. He is an interpreter of the secrets and stories inherent in the landscape, and a creator of forms which might express them.

Turning the pages of this endlessly absorbing book I am struck by its spirit of exploration and experiment. Topographical art has a reputation for playing rather safe, but look at the quiet audacity of Newdick's compositions. The focal point is often the gaping black hole of a barn entrance. Not many artists could pull that off. Nor would many take the risk of devoting nearly half a sheet to a stretch of chicken-wire fence, as Newdick does in drawing 64, honouring the idiosyncrasies of each little wire hexagon. The stone shed beyond it is cordoned off, unreachable, unsalvageable, its front window patched up like a bad eye. How then is this drawing so beguiling? Why do I want to look at it for hours? I feel the same about drawing 16, a redundant stable behind a fence. Its moods seem to be so various. The building stands up smartly, at the same time as falling down. The carefully quoined brickwork tells a different story from the utilitarian door with its triangular danger sign. It is a hotch-potch and it is a whole; it is a little ridiculous, what with that spruce tree apparently growing out of the roof, but it is also arrestingly beautiful.

Each building bears the marks of having changed over time: each has been repaired and adapted. So the drawings are records of long passages of time, and they are records, too, of the time Newdick spent working at each place. In the week or so it takes to make a drawing, all sorts of things can happen. Sometimes events go into the picture itself: a Chinook helicopter hovers weightily above a barn at Egdean. More often they go into the short texts which Newdick sees as integral to the drawings and in which he notes down the sounds of a passer-by, the vapour trails of planes, the similarity of silage to giant marshmallows, a problem with perspective, the punishing cold. These are tiny fragments of an artist's autobiography: life as it is lived while drawing. With his eyes on the barn, Newdick's thoughts leap off in all directions. The bubbles on a pond take him, elliptically, to 'a wet night and a long journey'; a late hogweed leads to paper doilies and a long-dead aunt. Memory is going back and forth; the Chinook is going to Afghanistan; the world opens out from here.

One barn, near Lurgashall, did not survive long enough to have its portrait finished: it collapsed between Newdick's first and second visits. Drawings 19 to 21 are therefore pictures of something that doesn't now exist. Perhaps that's why they feel a little more elegiac than the others, though they are without sentimentality. The timber framed interior in drawing 19 reminds me of a moment in Virginia Woolf's novel *Jacob's Room* when we listen to sounds in the emptiness: 'One fibre in the wicker arm-chair creaks, though no-one sits there'. The vaulted barn at Lurgashall seems to shift and stretch like that, as if the building were carrying on its own conversation. It may be empty, but it is moulded to the shape of the people who used it. Perhaps, if we look hard enough, something of the pattern of their lives can be traced, very faintly, in the cross-beams and rafters.

INTRODUCTION

On 28 January 1940 the *New York Times* reported that:

> "... for the first time [since] the war began, British censors today allowed that humdrum conversational topic, the weather, which has been a strict military secret in Britain, to be mentioned in news dispatches – providing the weather news is more than fifteen days old."

It may have been news to New York but the British did not need reminding. The winter of 1939–40 was the coldest for almost half a century. The River Thames was iced over between Teddington and Sunbury and at Bognor Regis the sea froze. Night temperatures as low as 20 degrees below freezing were frequently recorded and anyone reasonably fit and not too heavy could have skated the length of the Grand Union Canal from Birmingham to London.

But it was not ice skating that occupied the minds of the people, for on the mainland of Europe, Nazi Germany, with whom Britain had been at war for little more than three months, seemed already to be exercising an efficient authority as alarming in its way as was the weather at home. Their ice-cold and (though no-one cared to admit to this) stylish uniforms seemed to symbolise the threat and Britain was afraid.

While government and the military were planning defence strategies a team led by the Director of The National Gallery, Sir Kenneth Clark, and with funding from The Pilgrim Trust, set up a scheme intended to boost national morale[1] by employing artists to celebrate and record those aspects of the country's architectural and cultural heritage which were thought to be in imminent danger from bomb damage. The scheme, which was to become known as 'Recording Britain' would eventually lead to a collection of more than 1500 (mainly) watercolour drawings which are now in the care of the Victoria & Albert Museum in London. The artists were many and varied – from the unknown and unremarkable to established figures including Sir William Russell Flint and John Piper. (Though Piper, being Piper, seemed often to be more interested in the effects of weather than in tangible artefacts).[2] Unsurprisingly, while some of the work is undeniably first rate, much of it remains rather undistinguished though perhaps it is this aspect of the scheme that provides its charm and which would seem to say something of the 'make do and mend' approach to life that was imposed on Britain by conflict.

There is a certain irony in all of this. As things turned out and the stylish uniforms proved ultimately vulnerable, most of the Recording Britain subjects proved in their turn to survive the onslaught from overseas. What many of them did not survive, however, was the home grown threat from post war development, speculation, and road building and widening. Today that threat continues and in a time of upheaval and change (which, for those of us who are not economists and who value the idea of stability, seems often to be change for change's sake) the threat is, arguably, as arresting as the idea of invasion from a foreign power.

With these concerns to the fore and with the principle of Recording Britain for ever as a background I began, in the autumn of 2009, to work on a set of drawings of traditional farm buildings on the Leconfield Estate around Petworth in West Sussex. My subjects were not, of course, in danger from enemy action but from inevitable social and agricultural change and from nature and time itself. Nature is a key word and it is not easy to define. Most, though not all, of the buildings I worked on were in themselves pieces of nature: they were made, largely by hand, from natural materials – wood, stone, clay and not much more save for some lime and the odd bit of iron, and all of these would have come from close at hand. The building grew, or was made to grow, from the ground on which it stood – it became a natural extension of the land and I would define this branch of manufacture as a wholly natural one. In my view it is a construction whose principles are no different and no less a part of nature from those of the beaver's lodge, the termite's tower or the waxy hexagonals of the honey bee.

Gradually though, as farm machinery became ever larger, and without essential (and increasingly expensive) maintenance, many of these natural buildings would fall into disuse and ivies, brambles, docks, nettles and the ever present elder would come to over-run them and pull them back into the ground from which they were made. Ashes to ashes or natural recycling depending on your interpretation.

People have often inquired of me why, if this is an exercise in recording, I don't take photographs. In 1939 Kenneth Clark was asked the same question, replying that photographs offered 'fact' and that painting provided 'feeling'. I think I know what he was getting at but it's not really a good enough answer and I think too, that any self-respecting photographer would take issue with him. You have only to look at the photographs of Bill Brandt, who was working at the same time as Recording Britain to see that photography can, on the contrary, be all about feeling without the fact.

My initial answer to the question is even less convincing than Clark's: drawing is what I do and I'm not much of a photographer. But, going further, it is worth thinking about terminology. We 'take' a photograph but we 'make' a drawing. Using these established terms, a photograph becomes a sort of theft while a drawing is a form of giving. Again, photographers will object to this, but I think there is something in it and that something is to do with speed. It doesn't take long to take a photograph – you may have to wait a bit for the light to be right but hardly ever for the four or five days on which I am working at my drawing. Photography can be a sort of surreptitious act, sneaky even (and I am not talking about celebrities and paparazzi) but you cannot make a drawing without becoming an obvious part of the landscape you are in. It is important, I think, to become part of the landscape – to become, for a while at least, the landscape itself, just as the building I am drawing is part of the landscape and ultimately becomes nature itself.

Writing in *The Listener* in July 1941 the art historian Herbert Read echoes Clark's views on photography: "Photography can do much, but it cannot give us the colour and atmosphere of a scene, the intangible *genius loci*." He goes on to say that it is this intangible element which is so easily destroyed that "... shows us exactly what we are fighting for – a green and pleasant land, a landscape whose features have been moulded in liberty, whose every winding lane and irregular building is an expression of our national character." Read was dealing here with a sort of 'Englishness' which probably had developed more in the national consciousness or sub-consciousness than in life itself but nevertheless it was something with which many people in England could readily identify.

This sense of a sub-conscious Englishness seems still to prevail, if in a somewhat diluted and less identifiable form. It was something of which I was aware when I began my drawings around Petworth in 2009 and since I have expanded my range, both geographically and in terms of subject matter, it is a sense which I find I am sharing with others. In this era of rapid change, especially technological change, most people look for at least some sense of stability. Once it was only those of us who were cynical but now all but the most malleable of us have come to realise that the increasing pace of obsolescence has made a nonsense of so-called 'state of the art' artefacts like the iPad which are in fact outmoded even before they are launched on to an ever-gullible and over-rich public. What is there now to rely on? The past is a fairly safe bet. You have only to look at what we are offered by television companies and along with programmes about food and cooking (these a form of escapism as much as instruction) we are given endless popular insights into the activities of our ancestors, from *Timewatch* through *Who do you think you are?* to *Dad's Army*. There is security here and it is the same sort of security we find in old buildings. It's not new. In Anthony Trollope's *Barchester Towers* (1857) Mr Arabin, before proposing to Eleanor in the gardens at Ullathorne, says "There is something about old-fashioned mansions, built as this is, and old-fashioned gardens, that to me is especially delightful." To which she replies: "I like everything old-fashioned; old-fashioned things are so much the honestest."

Am I then dealing with 'honesty'? Perhaps. Certainly I am not a dealer in nostalgia, which is something that really has no place at all in what I am trying to do. If these drawings of mine are about anything they are about values – and I do mean 'values' not 'value' – there is a world of difference between the two. Many of the buildings on which I have worked have practically no value in the financial sense at all: most, thankfully, are not even suitable for conversion into bijou residences and a little bit of Chelsea in the countryside. Their inherent values, on the other hand are, for me at least, endless.

Honesty, perhaps; nostalgia, never. And what about heritage? It's a minefield. My wife, Fulvia, who comes from Venice, once said to me in a conversation about the National Trust, "In England they put railings around it but where I come from the boys play football against it." It was a provocative statement but she had a point: should we really be preserving all this stuff and protecting it or is it more honest to interact with it? Is it more sensible, more practical (and a damn site cheaper) to record it and let nature take its course? But at the same time to keep a repository of knowledge for the day when we really do lose our way and don't know where to turn.

In *The Heritage Industry* (1987) Robert Hewison suggested that heritage was bogus history and that we should be developing a critical culture to engage in a dialogue between past and present. Hewison and Fulvia, each in their way, are making the same case, I think. Some of the buildings I have been drawing over the past couple of years are falling down (one, catalogue numbers 19, 20 and 21, even collapsed during the period I was drawing it, though thankfully I was not in it at the time). This seems to me to be the proper order of things. Buildings die. People die. It is sad, often it is heartbreaking, and you don't get over it – you learn to live with it. And we should all learn to live with the impermanence of nature but at the same time see impermanence as a detail within a continuity which may be God-given or not, depending on our individual beliefs.

I will consider this exercise as a success if, when it is over, it is seen as a set of well-judged, worthwhile drawings each of which might have the ability to arouse emotions in its viewers. If, at the same time, my task contributes a little to the repository of traditional technologies, then that is an additional bonus.

A method of working

I have often said that I do not make drawings *of* things; I make drawings *about* things. Indeed, when galleries ask me to provide an 'artist's statement' (a concept with which I am wholly unsympathetic and which inevitably results in some constructed pretentious claptrap), the *of* and *about* phrase is all I will reveal. So how should I make a drawing about values and honesty which are wrapped up in landscape and buildings?

The first thing is to take a lot of photographs. This is not a contradiction of the views of Kenneth Clark and Herbert Read and 'photographs' is probably the wrong word anyway. 'Snaps' would be better. The purpose of these is to establish viewpoints and to determine the boundaries of the picture. Traditionally, artists would carry pieces of cardboard with rectangular holes cut in them and hold them up between the eye and the view but it was all a bit hit and miss. Far better to take some snaps. Back at home I put them into the computer, crop them and print the likely candidates – perhaps one, perhaps half a dozen. I then copy the basic shapes and proportions on to my drawing paper and return to the site, usually the following day. The photograph is now of no further use. It's in the bin, the camera is back in its box and the pictures in the computer are clicked away to the trash.

Back on site I find the right place and sit on my little stool with my drawing board and my paper and pencils – the paper is Fabriano 300gm/^{2} smooth and I use 0.3HB, 0.5HB and 0.5B clutch pencils. At first I just sit there looking, breathing the perfumes, listening. Perhaps I will go for a little walk, perhaps touch and feel the thing I am making the drawing about. Tentative. Making discoveries. It's like shaking hands, a nervous meeting. This thing is bigger and stronger than I am. I feel like a lion tamer.

Text

Recording Britain was a national scheme through which artists produced watercolour pictures. My exercise is essentially local and the drawings are all in pencil. Other than these, the chief difference between what I am doing now and what was done in the second world war is that each of my pictures is accompanied by a piece of writing. These paragraphs, which range from four to about 200 words, are written on site as the drawing is being made, sometimes at the side of the picture (see the cover illustration) or in my notebook. They are not intended to serve as captions nor are they necessarily subordinate to the drawings – they act as extensions to them. I see no intellectual difference between writing and drawing, each being a form of the other and each is suited to a particular aspect of emotional expression or recording.

Considered inaccuracies and a lack of people

In the drawing of the barn at Lickfold (catalogue number 54) there is a dense little wood of trees on the right hand side which could almost be the edge of a forest. These trees do not exist, or rather they do exist but not here. There are other instances: I am not averse to manipulating landscape, to adding and taking away – this, after all, is the great advantage that I have over the photographer and I'm not going to forfeit it. However, with regard to the buildings, I only rarely make adjustments to what I see.

As well as adjusting landscape to suit my drawings I also remove its people. Inevitably, as I work on a picture someone will wander into my field of view but they never go into the drawings. I don't need more people. They are there already. I see them everywhere. Every brick I look at, every stone, each sawn weather-board or cleft tie-beam, these all carry signs of life, from the carpenters' numbering of the timber joints to chisel marks on masonry. Although I am aware of all these people, the long dead artisans and craftsmen, the labourers and yeomen, I doubt that anyone looking at my drawings will be. They are hard to discern unless you are there in person. And of course there are traces of contemporary life too – tyre marks in shallow snow and the deep ruts of tractor tyres in thick mud.

Printmaking

I wonder sometimes why I am making these rather traditional, perhaps old-fashioned topographical drawings. Much of my work involves printmaking (especially etching) and investigating ways of making monoprints[3] – graphite and solvent transfer – and often the results have little to do with landscape or buildings and they are never topographical. The solvent transfer 'Laura, 1640'

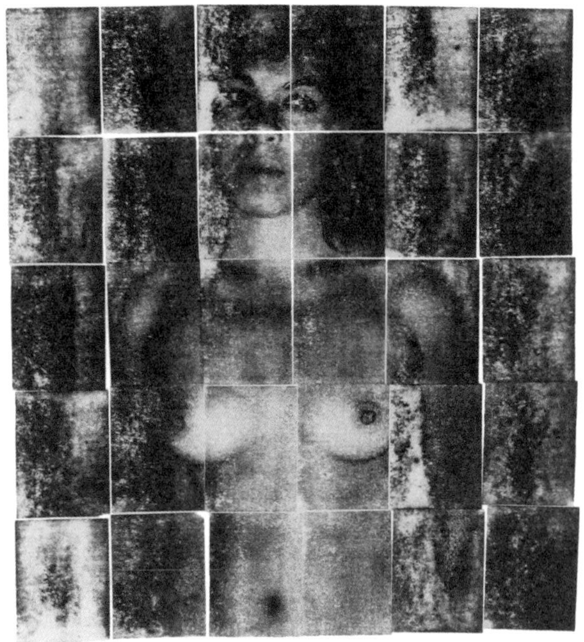

Jonathan Newdick, 'Laura, 1640'. Solvent transfer on paper, 42.0 × 36.0 cm., 2010. (Private collection).

is an example. Visual art, though, is about an appreciation of what ideas *might* look like and about what artefacts *do* look like and for the second of these I have not found a better way of keeping the eyes in trim than by looking at something and trying to draw it. On the whole you tend to draw what excites you or what interests you. I was a child among the sort of buildings I am looking at here, I watched my father working among them and they have become not only a part of my history but a part of my present too. That history and this present are half a century apart but, like identical transparencies, if you carefully overlap them and hold them up to the light they make one picture. More than this, it is a picture with an added dimension. Perhaps a bit fuzzy here and there but a picture which, while it may not have three dimensions, clearly has more than two.

Jonathan Newdick, Petworth, 2012

1. It would seem to me that Clark is straying into risky territory here. The idea of boosting national morale by pointing out what the country could lose as the result of enemy action could have the reverse effect. It was hoped, of course, that it might heighten peoples' determination to do what they could to deter what would become known as 'the Nazi war machine' and give them a reason to fight.

2. There is a nice anecdote concerning Piper's enjoyment of foreboding skies and threatening weather. At the same time as he was working on his Recording Britain pictures he was asked by the Queen (later H.M. The Queen Mother), by way of Kenneth Clark, to make some watercolours of Windsor Castle. Working often in winter under glowering skies and shunning cheery spring weather he produced twenty-six watercolours which seem to set the tone for his later designs for the theatre. When they were shown to the King, a man with perhaps less acute artistic sensibilities than those of his wife, he remarked "You seem to have very bad luck with your weather, Mr Piper."

3. By 'monoprint' I mean a print or a transfer which is made with or without using a printing press and from which only one image can be made. The usual term for this technique is 'monotype' but I don't use the word: it can be confused with 'Monotype' (with a capital initial). This refers to the Monotype Corporation, founded in 1887, suppliers of typesetting machinery and of type, including Bell 341 in which this book is set.

CATALOGUE

All works are pencil on paper and all were made between 2009 and 2012. Sizes are given in centimetres, height before width and in each case the reproduction size is 42 per cent of the size of the original.

All locations are in West Sussex and 44 of the drawings were made on sites where there is no public access. These are given imprecise titles (all containing the word 'near') to protect the privacy of the owners, tenant farmers, gamekeepers and others who live and work there. Drawings made on the remaining sites are accessible from roads, footpaths and other rights of way and these are given more precise titles.

The following drawings are not included in the exhibition at the Weald and Downland Open-air Museum in 2012: catalogue numbers 3, 18, 29, 31, 32, 34, and 51.

I

Field barn near
Petworth (1)
23.8 × 33.7 cm.

"Civilisation is on the operating table and we sit in the waiting room ..." – Cyril Connolly writing in the first issue of *Horizon* in 1937. It is easy today after the first decade of the new century to echo those words and they will drift like an ill breeze through these drawings. Sometimes it seems that someone has locked the waiting room door.

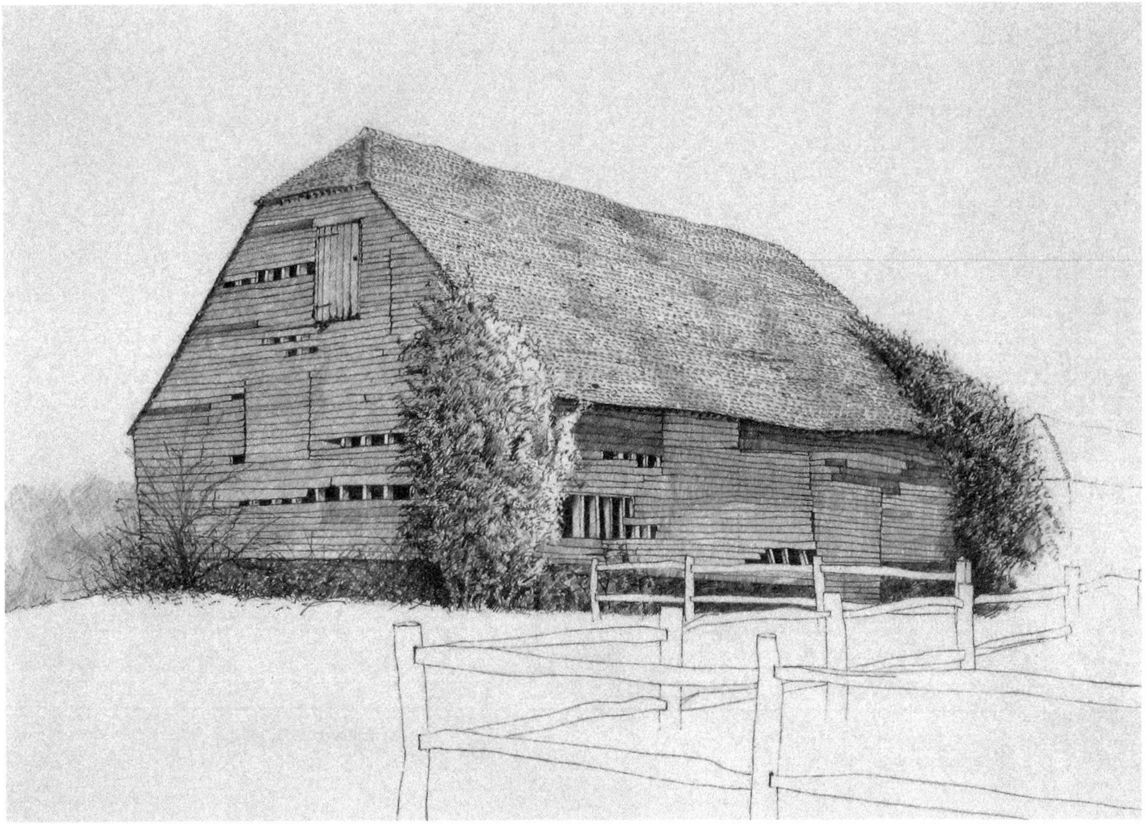

2

Field barn near
Petworth (2)
28.5 × 39.6 cm.

The sense of peace does not negate the determination to make discoveries. Like a private detective, his hat pulled down to hide his eyes. Or like some magus searching for an infant.

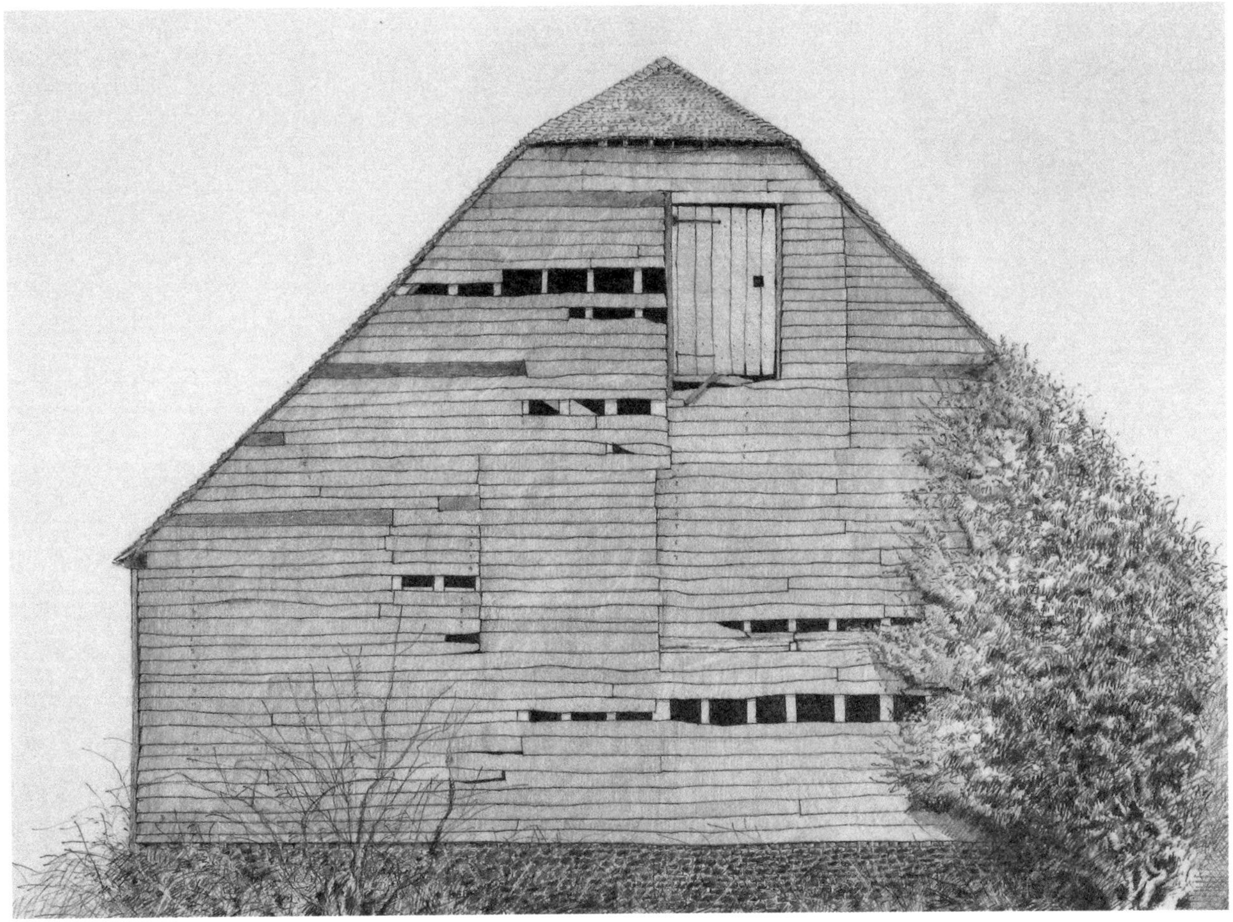

3

Field barn near Byworth
25.0 × 47.0 cm.
(Private collection)

Unless you are very careful, very vigilant, an excess of technology works against creativity. Confuses the issue. I'm not taking any risks – two pencils today (HB and 2B), a sheet of good Italian paper and a home-made stool to sit on. This is such a rare, bright and beautiful day, why should I need any more?

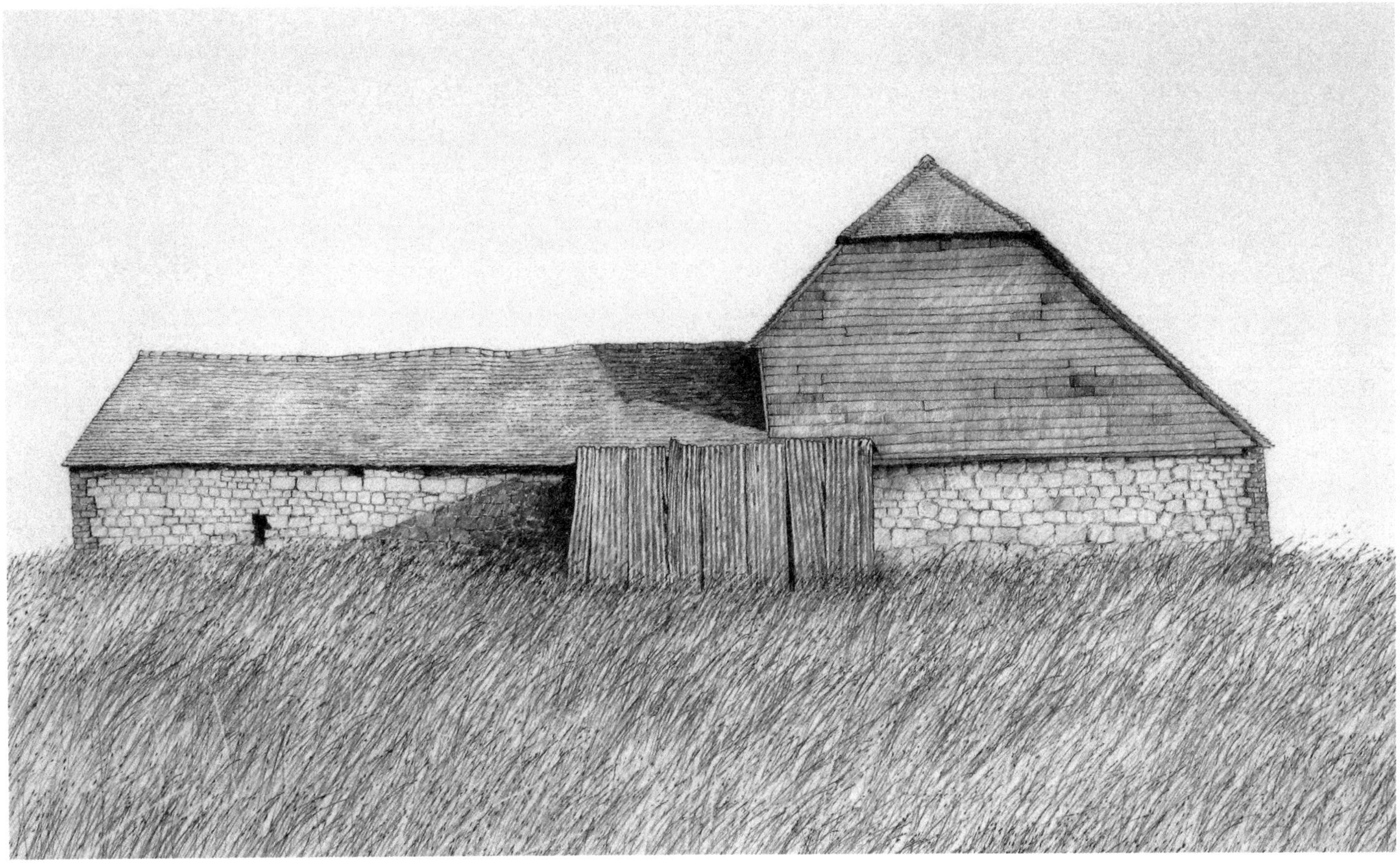

4

Cart shed at Glatting Farm, Sutton
30.0 × 42.6 cm.

A song thrush sits on the wire and says
everything twice, as if missed it the first time.
I didn't.

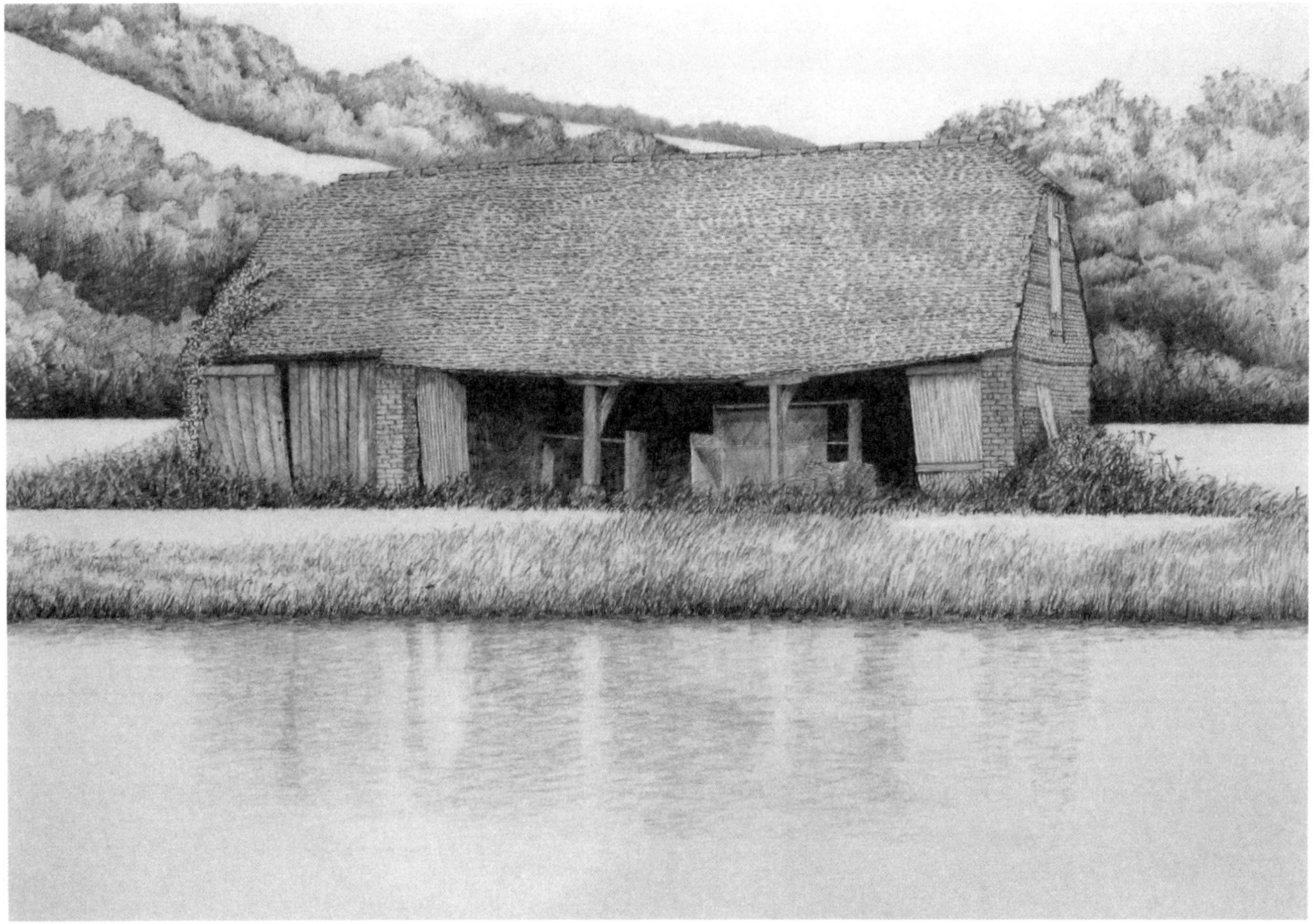

5

Barn at Glatting Farm, Sutton 28.0 × 50.8 cm.

Talking to the drawing. That line can't go there, surely. It seems to be right but if it stays there what should I do with this line here? Is this one right? Do I erase it? No, never that. Keep it. It'll tell a story. Or a lie.

Talking to my father. As a reader of Adrian Bell and a Man of the Fields himself he would have approved of this, I think. I hope so. Would my father have chosen between lines that lie and truthful lines? Would such distinctions have mattered to him?

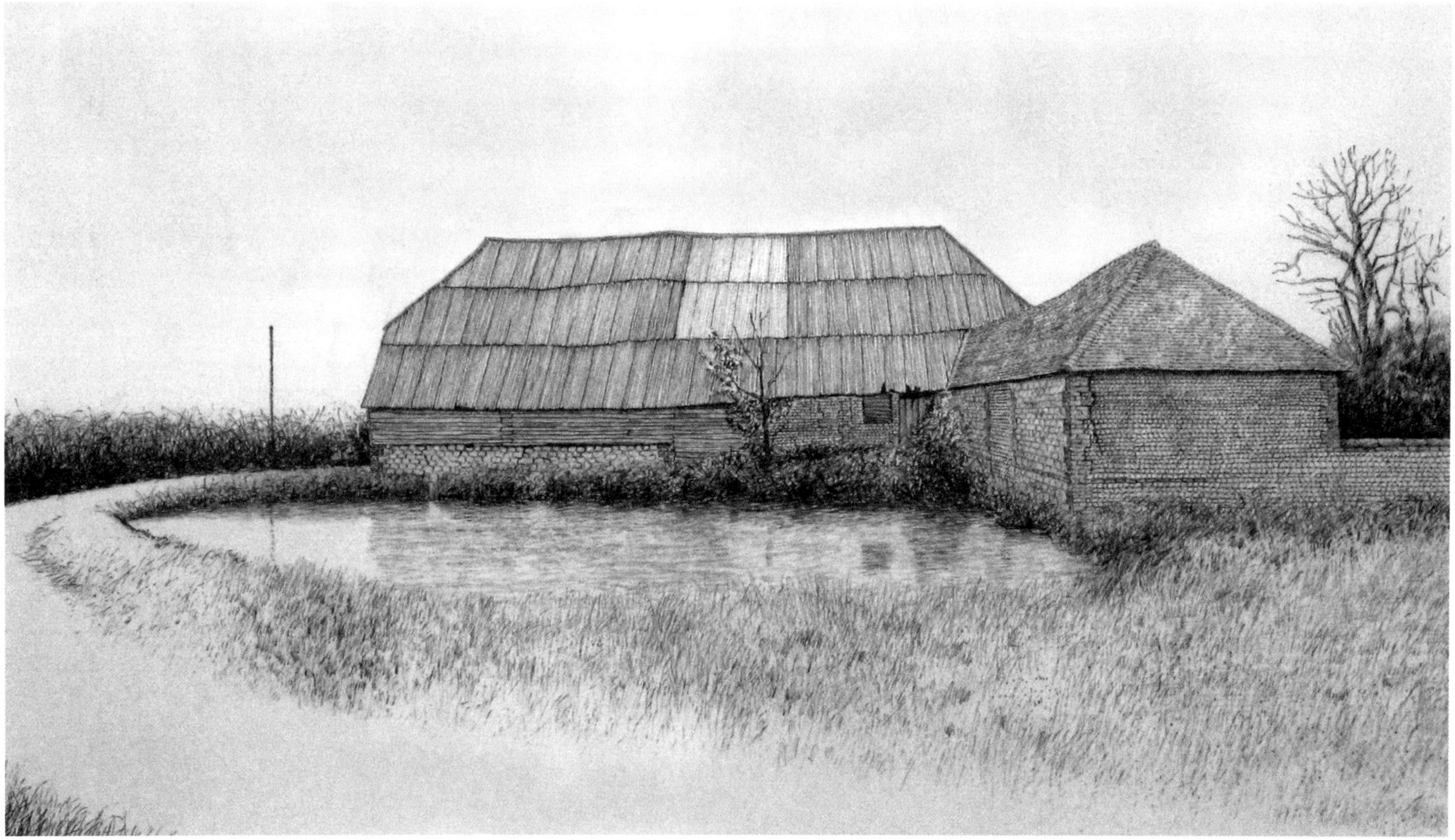

6

Outbuilding at Glatting Farm, Sutton
29.0 × 44.8 cm.

The wind in the wires sounds like a distant musician practising for the Mount Airy Fiddlers' Convention in North Carolina. In a galvanised fence post there are holes where the bolts should be. As it blows across these it reminds me of the Memphis Jug Band on a difficult day. These two together are almost there, but there is no rhythm section. There is rain though and I begin to see the practical value of watercolour over graphite. I pull my coat over my head and drawing board and in my little tent I am given the percussion. Who needs iTunes and a plug in your ear?

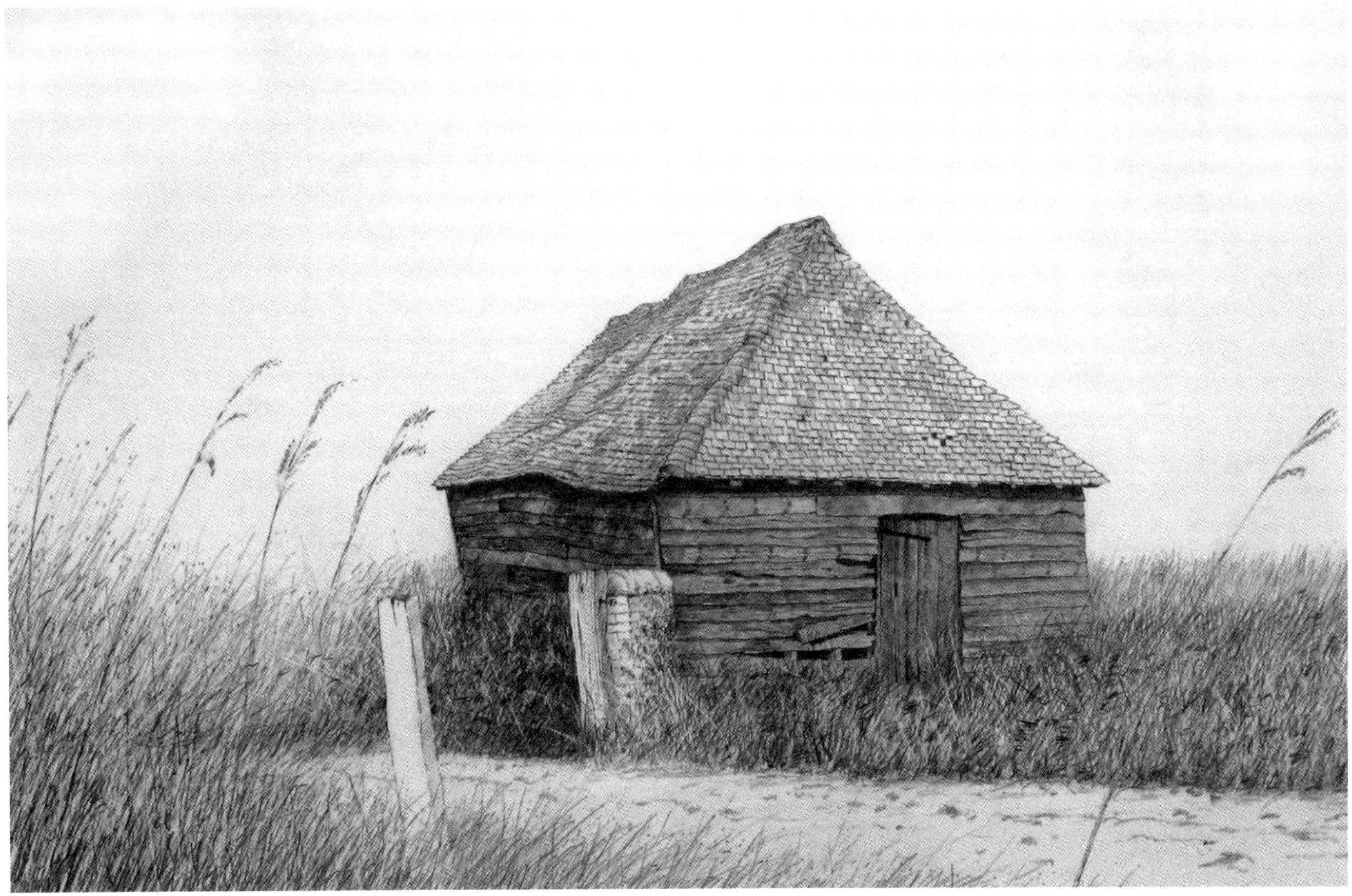

7

Glatting Farmhouse, Sutton
29.7 × 42.0 cm.

Cars. You can't trust cars. You get used to them being there and then they go away. Then as you are filling the void they left for you they return – but to a different place.

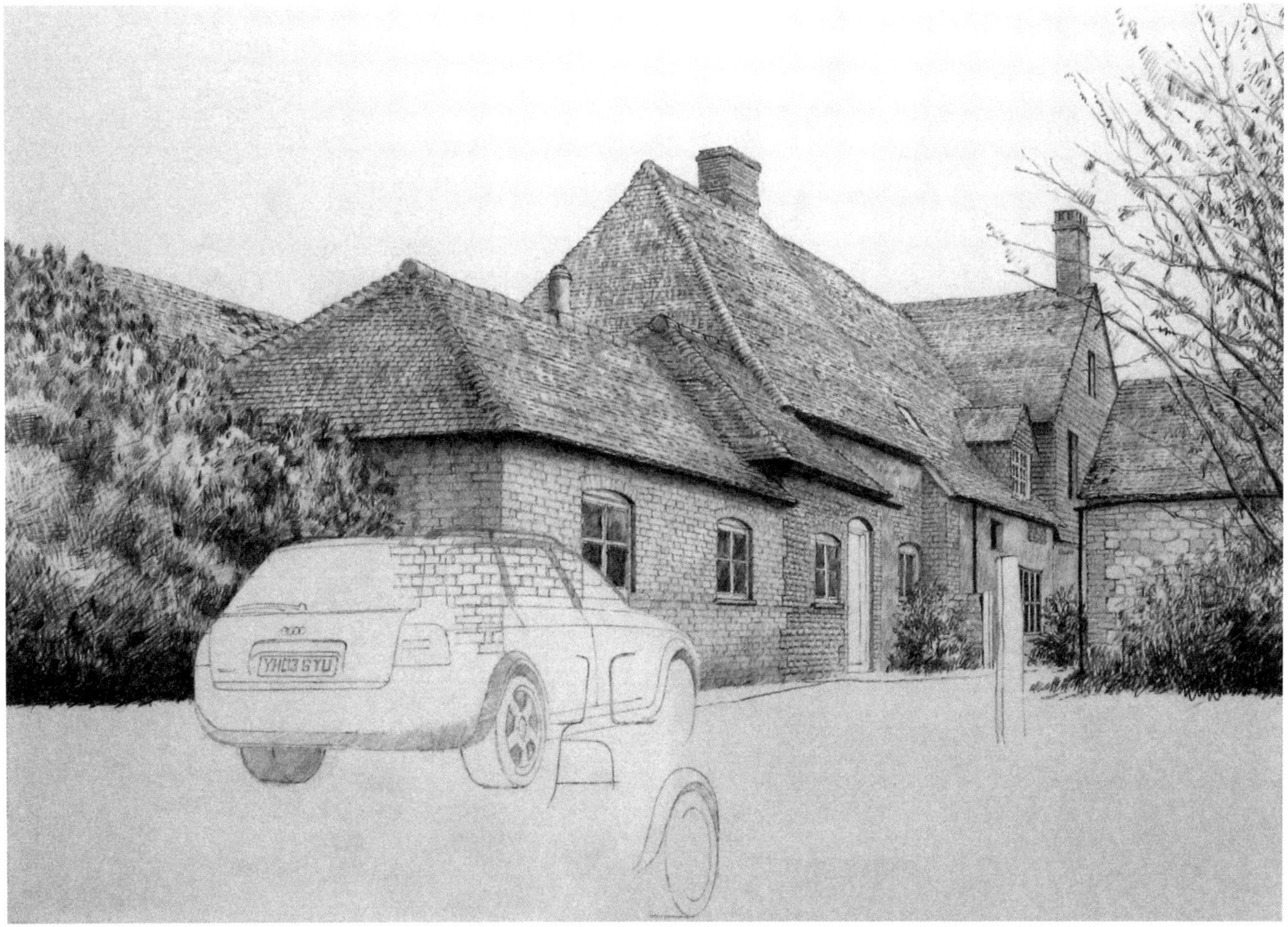

8

Timber framed barn
and stock yard next to
Barlavington Church
29.0 × 45.8 cm.

Drawing with a ruler. Class three at primary school and Miss Galloway said "Jonathan, real artists never use a ruler." And I believed her. I believed everything she said, her lovely hair in a golden bun, the perfume that my mother never wore. And where is she now, Miss Galloway?
I see her hair now, grey and silver and gathered more into a bird's nest than a bun. I still miss her but she was wrong about rulers. A handy tool, the ruler – not for drawing straight lines which always end up sterile. But good for marking distances on verticals and measuring things. Very good for that.

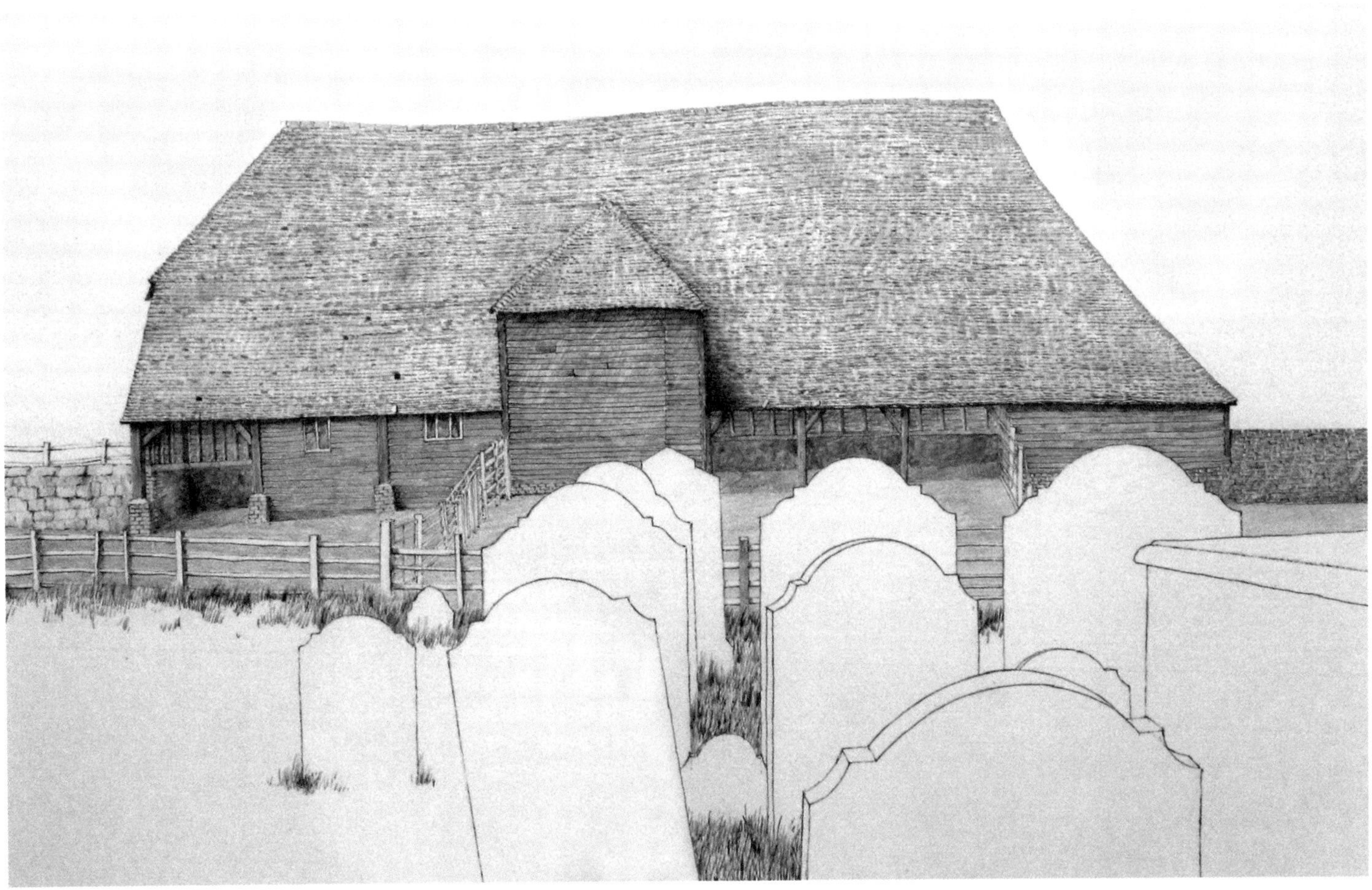

9

Stone barn on the River Rother near Petworth (1)
26.7 × 42.3 cm.

No, they are not architectural drawings although I acknowledge they may appear so. They are landscape drawings, for these buildings do not diminish the land. They don't even merely compliment it – they enhance it. They grow not only from the physical elements of the land but from the requirements and demands of a people whose lives were part of its natural rhythms and cycles.

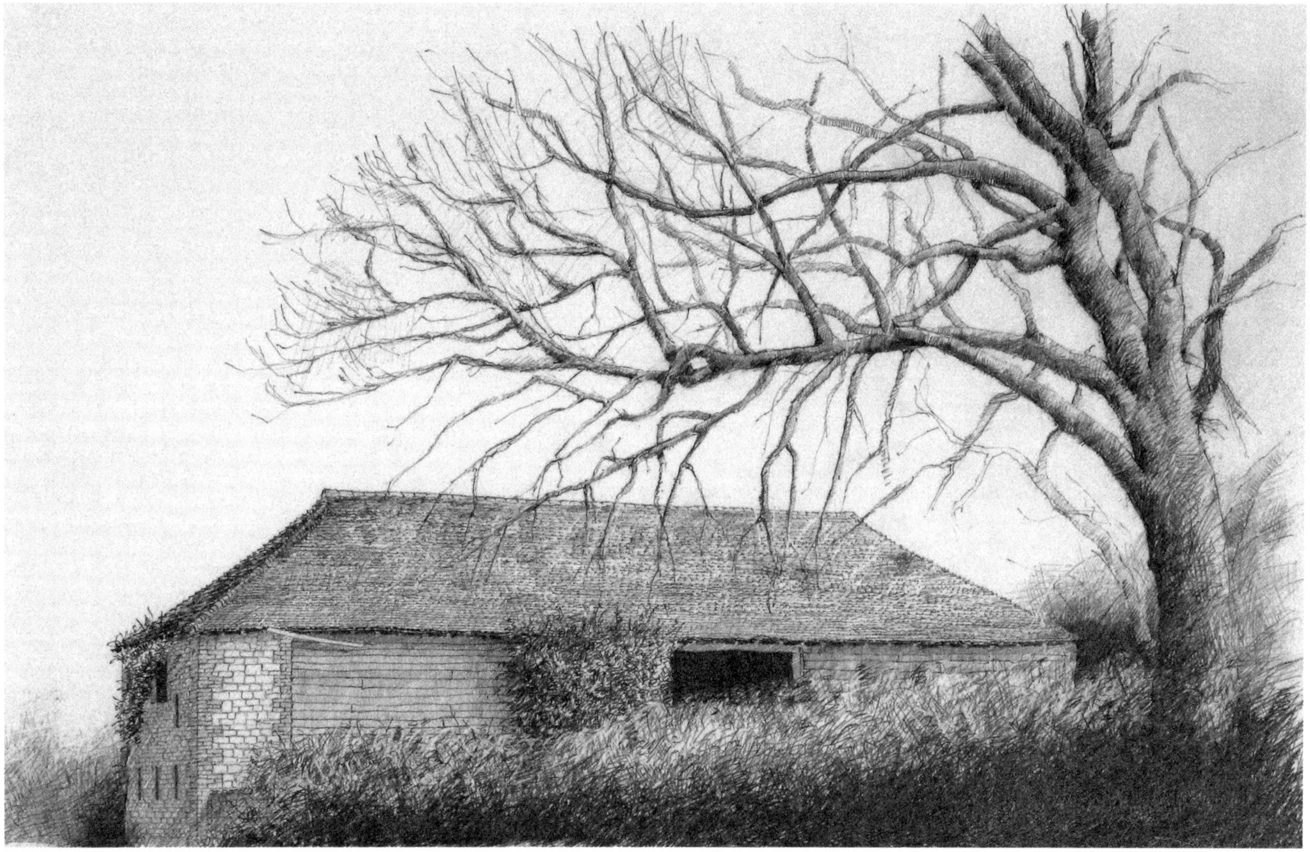

10

Stone barn on the River Rother near Petworth (2)
28.7 × 42.8 cm.

Rain. Deep water. Wellington boots. In the lane a white pick-up throws spray high above the hedges and you can't help thinking of a lifeboat bashing through the waves to those in peril.

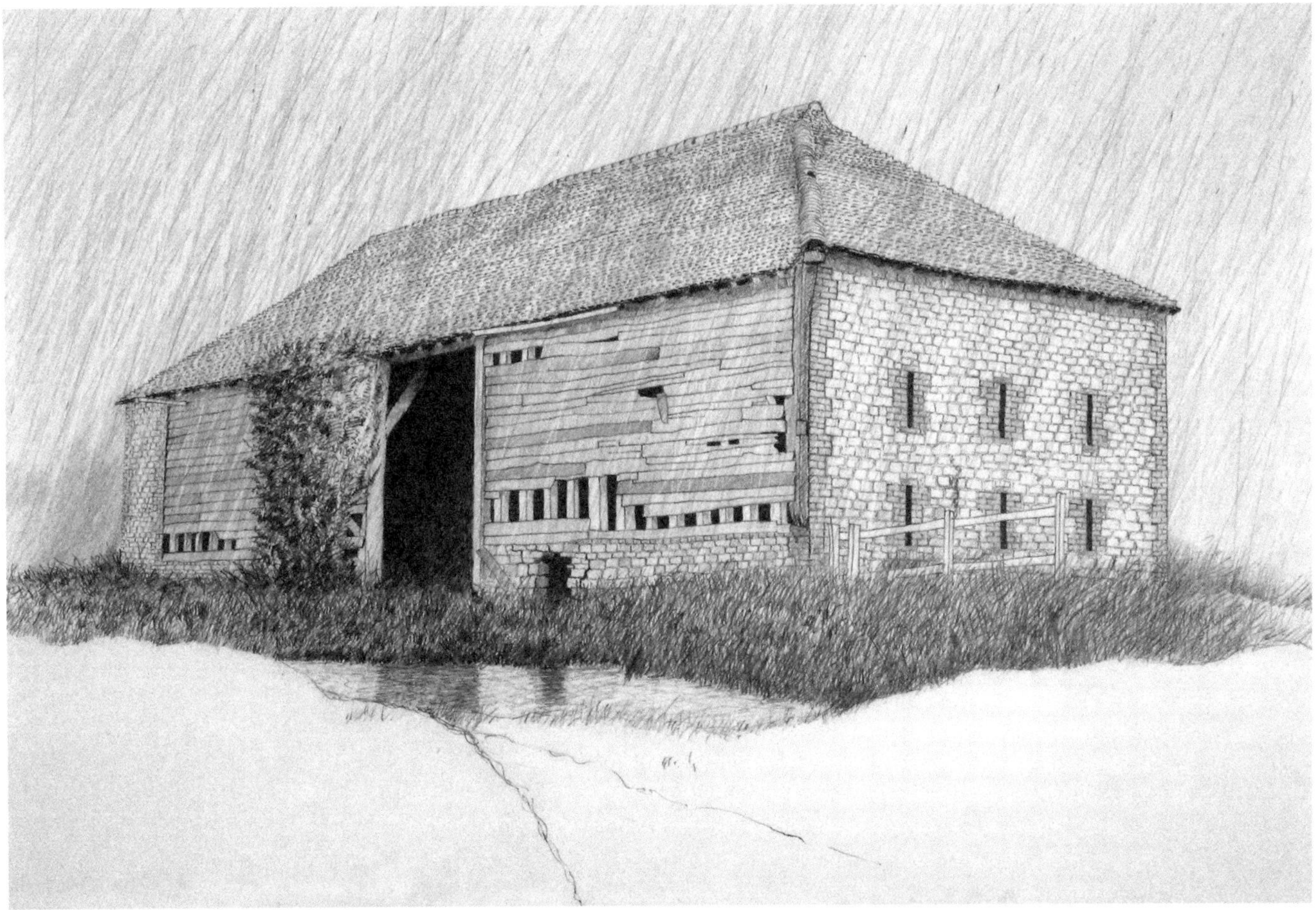

11

Abandoned farm buildings on the River Rother near Petworth
25.8 × 42.0 cm.

Sometimes these pencil lines are dull, like lead, and heavy. Sometimes they shine like pewter. They seem to reflect the weather.

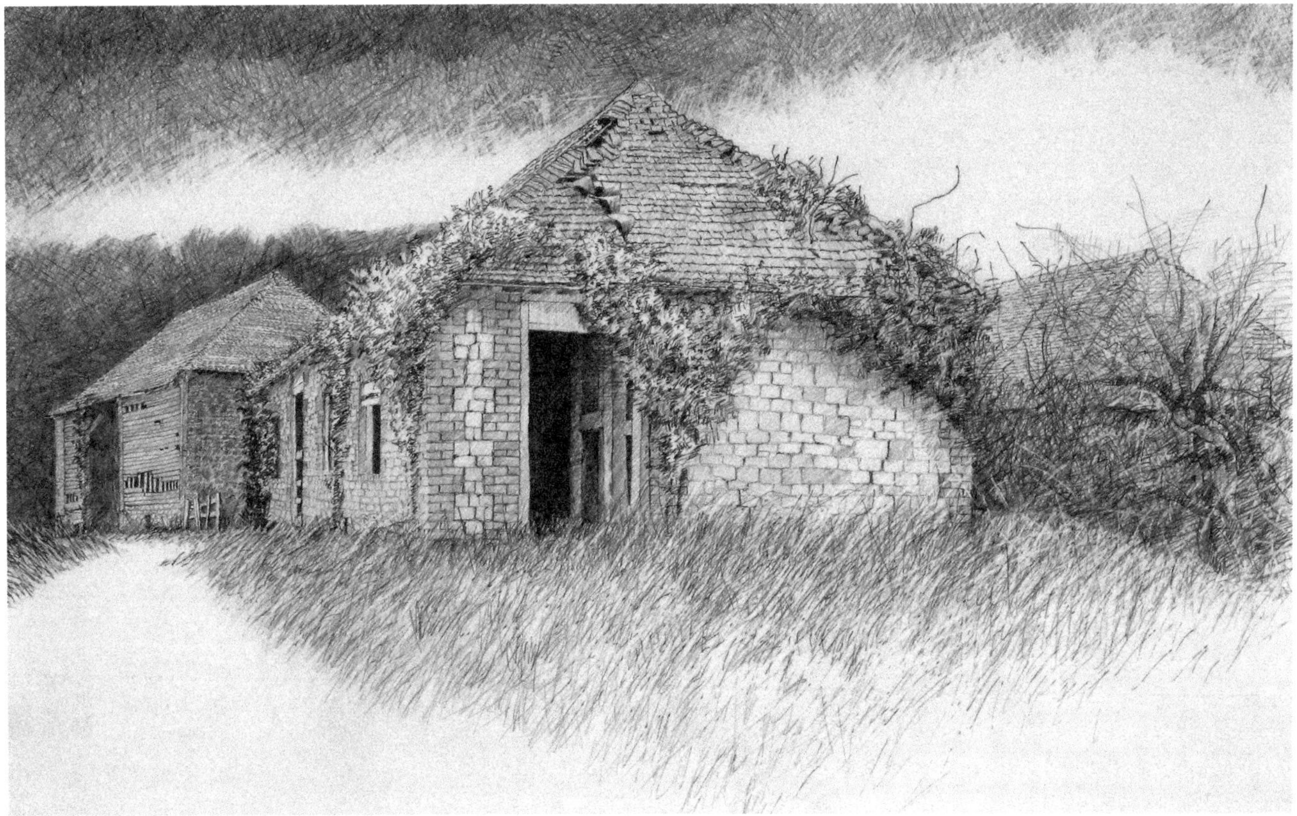

12

Stone barn on the River Rother near Petworth (3)
26.7 × 42.3 cm.

There is always the awkward question of what should be done with a redundant farm building. "It'd make a lovely house," they say. But, unlike warehouses overlooking St Catherine's Dock, or the East India, they don't acclimatise well to domesticity. Black pvc downpipes and anonymous factory-made windows (designed to enhance any building but doing the opposite to every building they are forced into). A garden made of gravel, of no use for anything but the parking of a BMW. These are always insulting to the original buildings and to the men who made and worked in them.

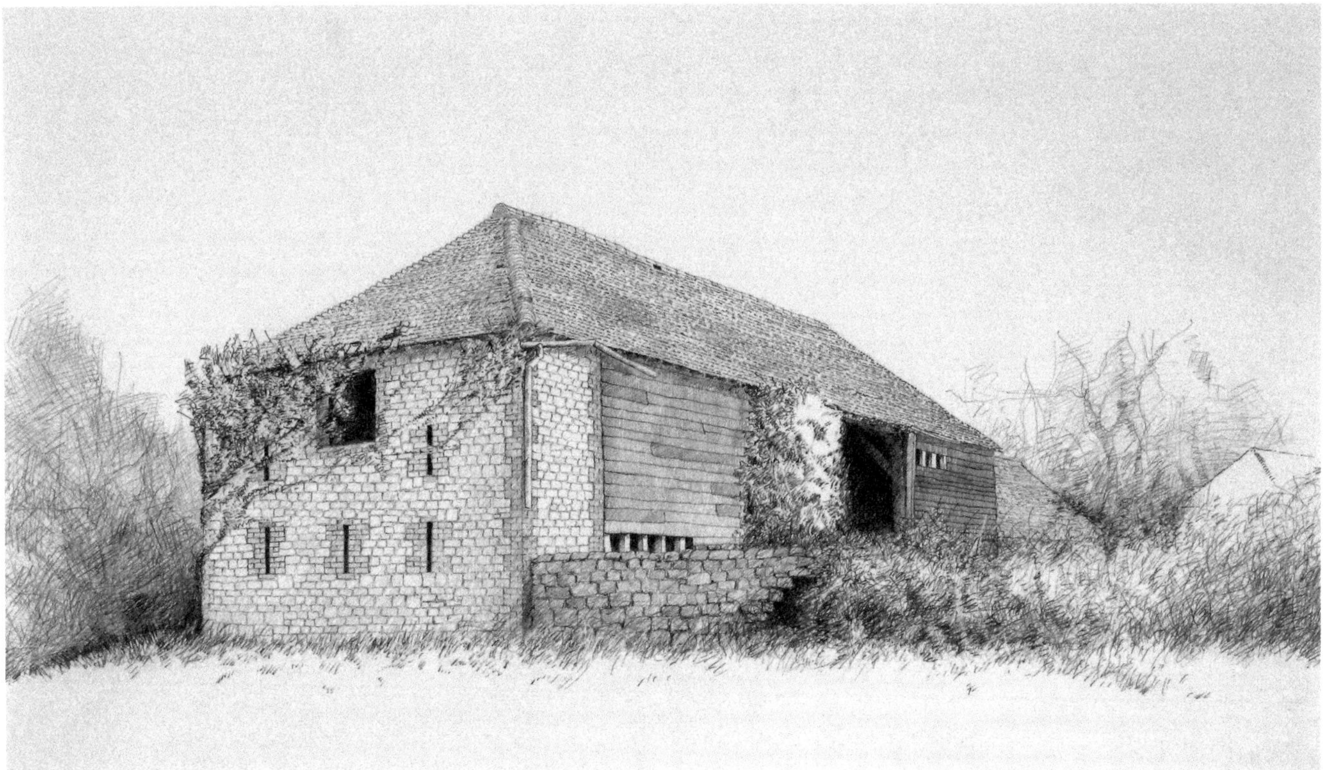

13

Dutch barn near Petworth
25.5 × 42.5 cm.

Skylarks singing in the endless blue sky. You almost never see them. To the poet the lark is 'she', to the ornithologist the lark is 'he' but to me, being neither of these it's 'it' and it gives me hope.

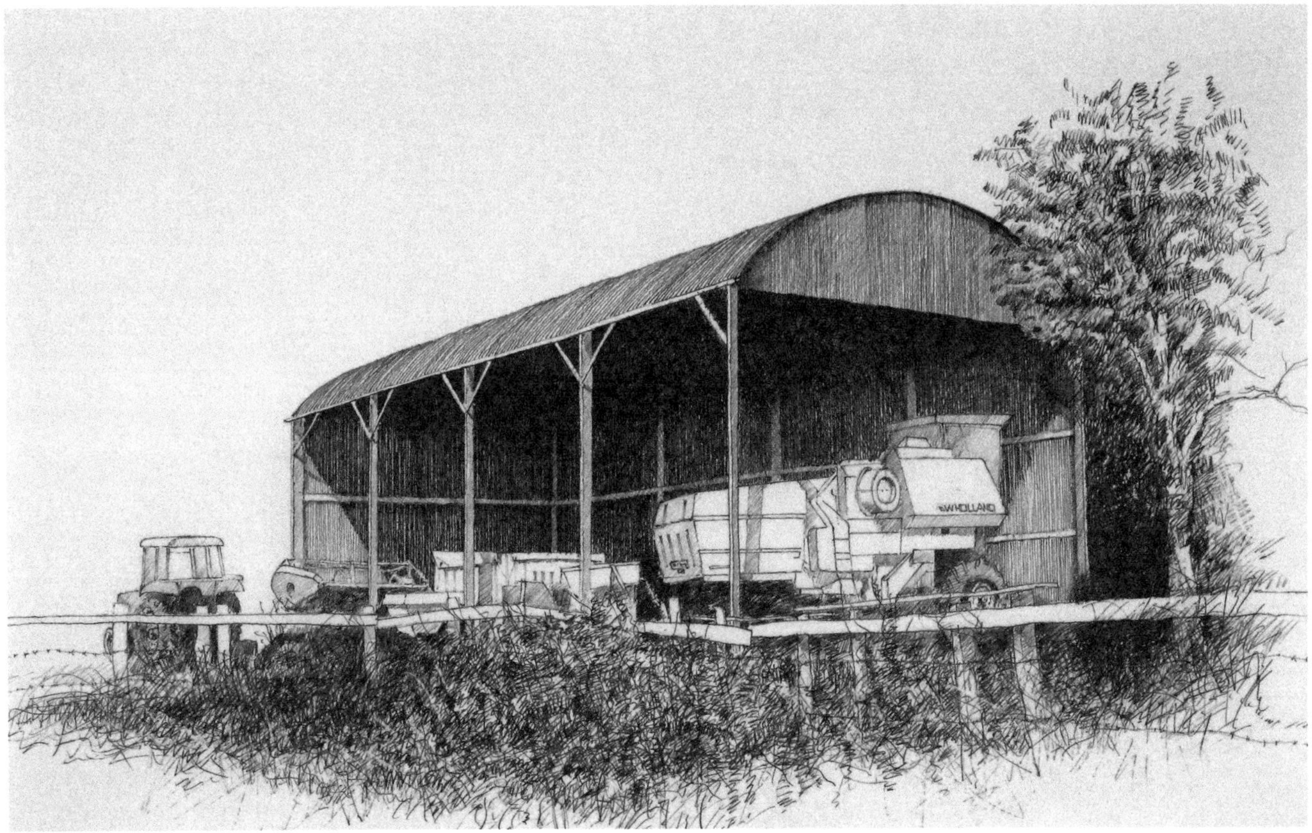
HOLLAND

14

Farm buildings under
repair near Petworth
29.5 × 40.0 cm.

The eastern European workers have been planting lettuces all night. The lights of their big machinery sweep across the bedroom walls when they get to the end of the row. By morning the field which yesterday was bare brown earth has become green with lettuces. As snow, unannounced, makes everything white.

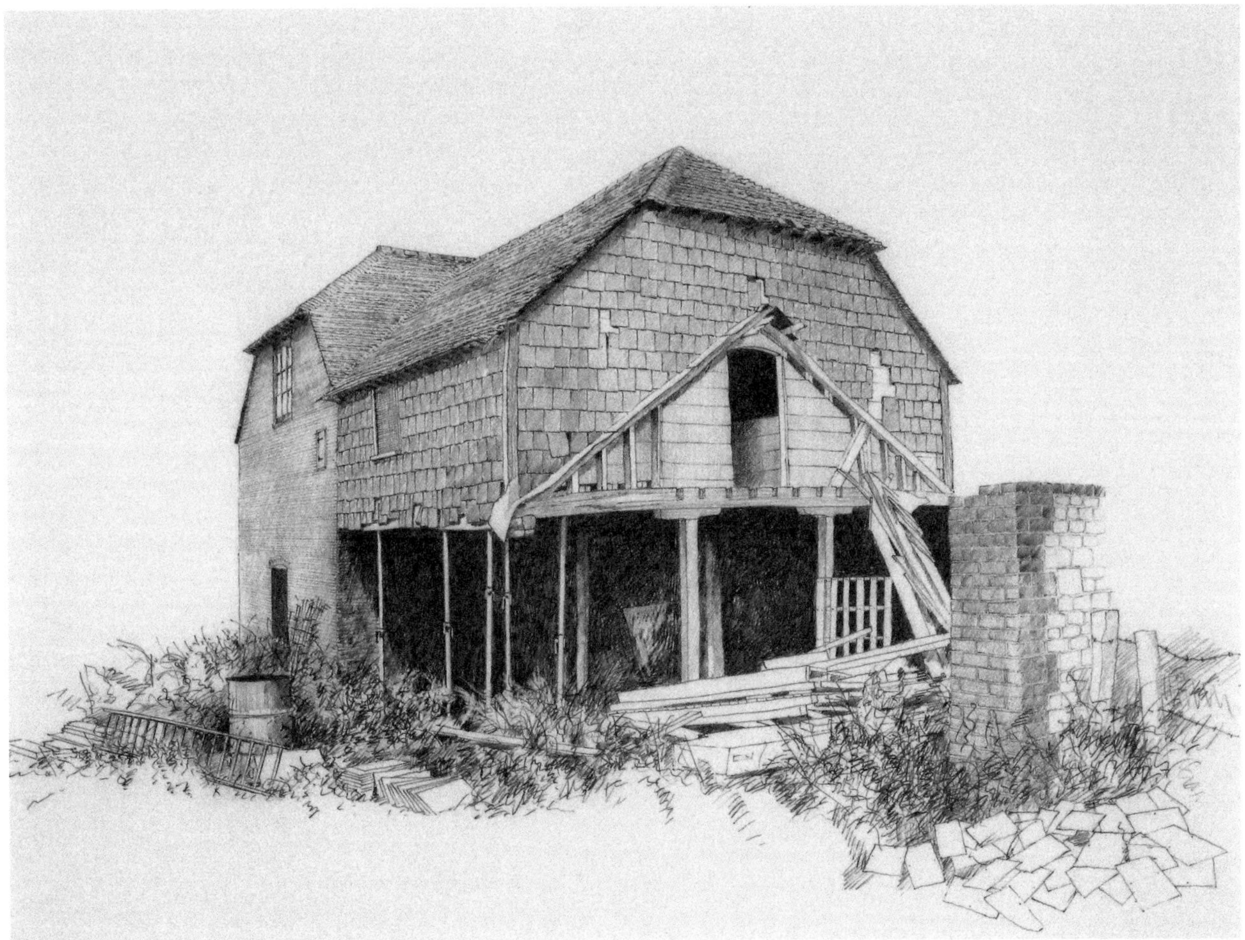

15

Farm buildings near Petworth
27.7 × 43.8 cm.

The railway used to run near here – bluebells and ransoms at the edge in spring. In summer Canadian fleabane and Oxford ragwort on the hot shale. Someone sitting unsteadily on a musty, patterned seat in third class, a brown paper parcel in the netting rack. On his way home to tea – meat and potatoes in the poor light of the parlour.

It's quieter here now. At first the dog barks but he knows me by now and it's merely a gesture. Half-hearted.

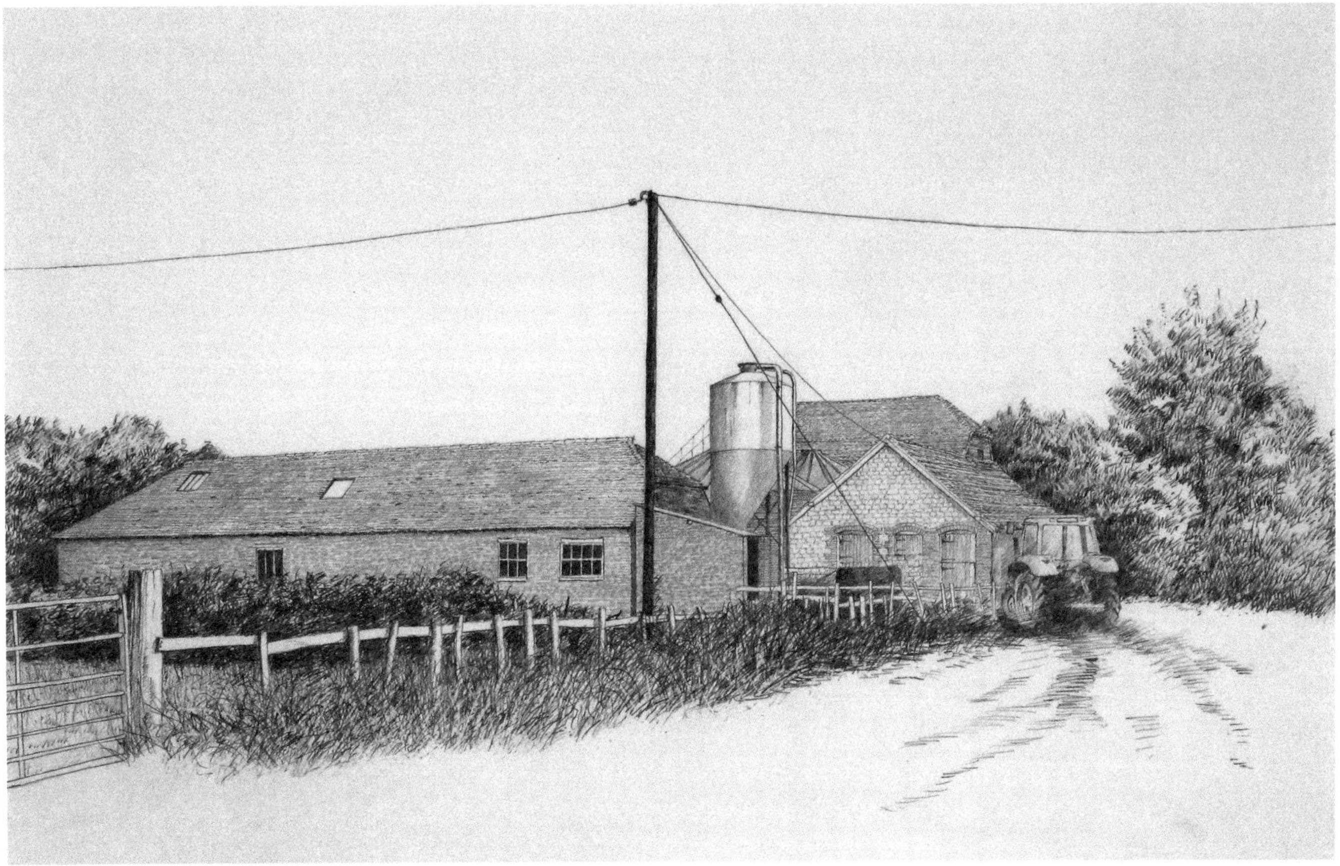

16

Redundant stable near Petworth
30.8 × 40.0 cm.

I am not going to draw the vapour trails. This morning it is as if all the airlines of the world, now allowed once again to fly, have combined to defeat Eyjafjallajökull at its own game.

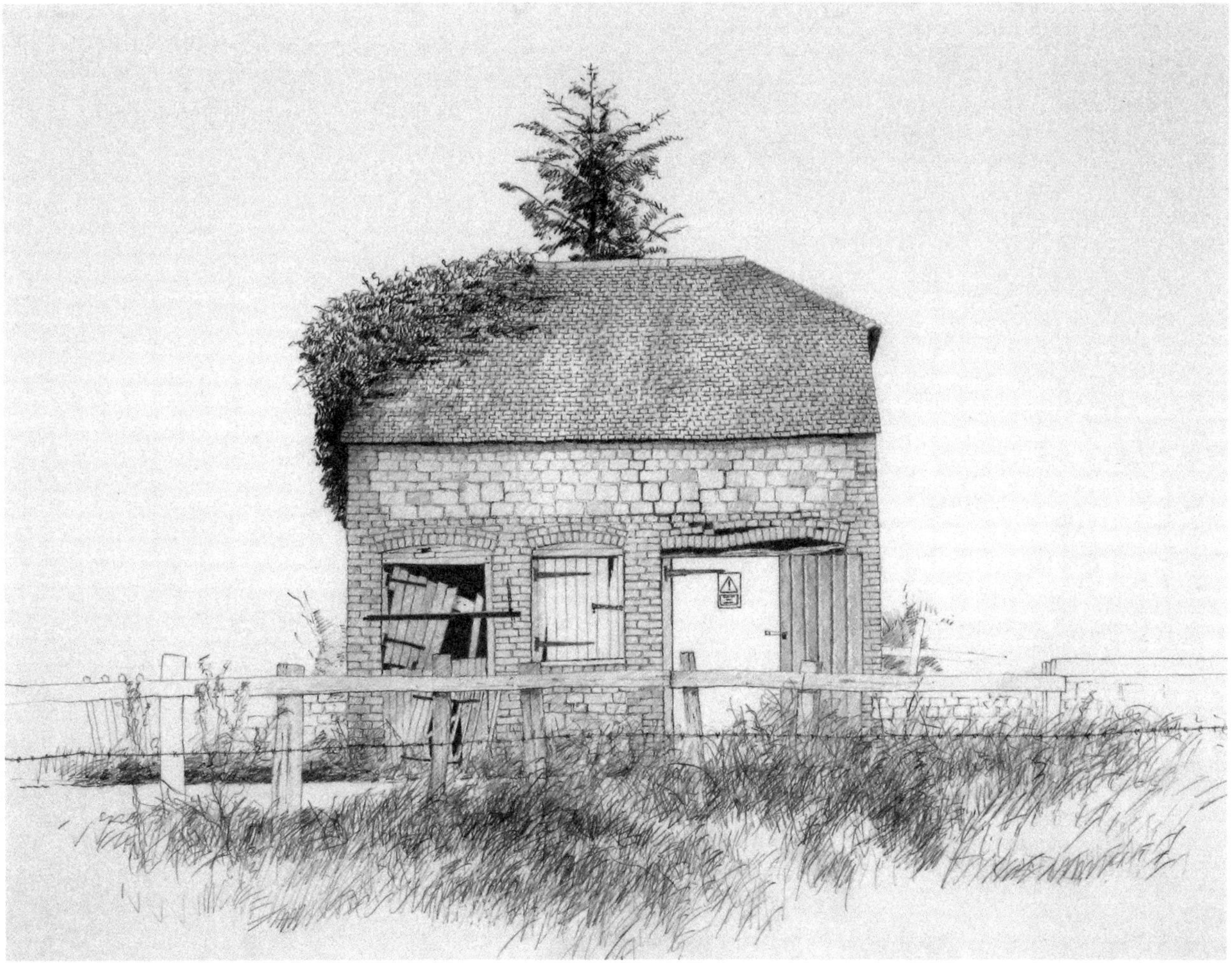

17

Abandoned cottages
near Lurgashall
27.6 × 41.2 cm.

A Keiller's Dundee marmalade jar, its white glaze cracked like rusting wire. Milk bottles in the mossy earth. They've gone green above but below, under the soil, they remain clear, clean, good as new.

Lily-of-the-valley, Solomon's seal are not discouraged by bramble and dock.

How long since anyone lived here? Thirty years perhaps. Perhaps longer. And yet they are here still. Welcoming, in a way. As you would welcome them if they were to return this early spring morning to interrupt your drawing.

And when the house is gone but for some stones, some Bakelite light fittings, a kettle perhaps, the flowers they planted will remain undiscouraged spring after spring. Each autumn an orchard of brambles and damsons.

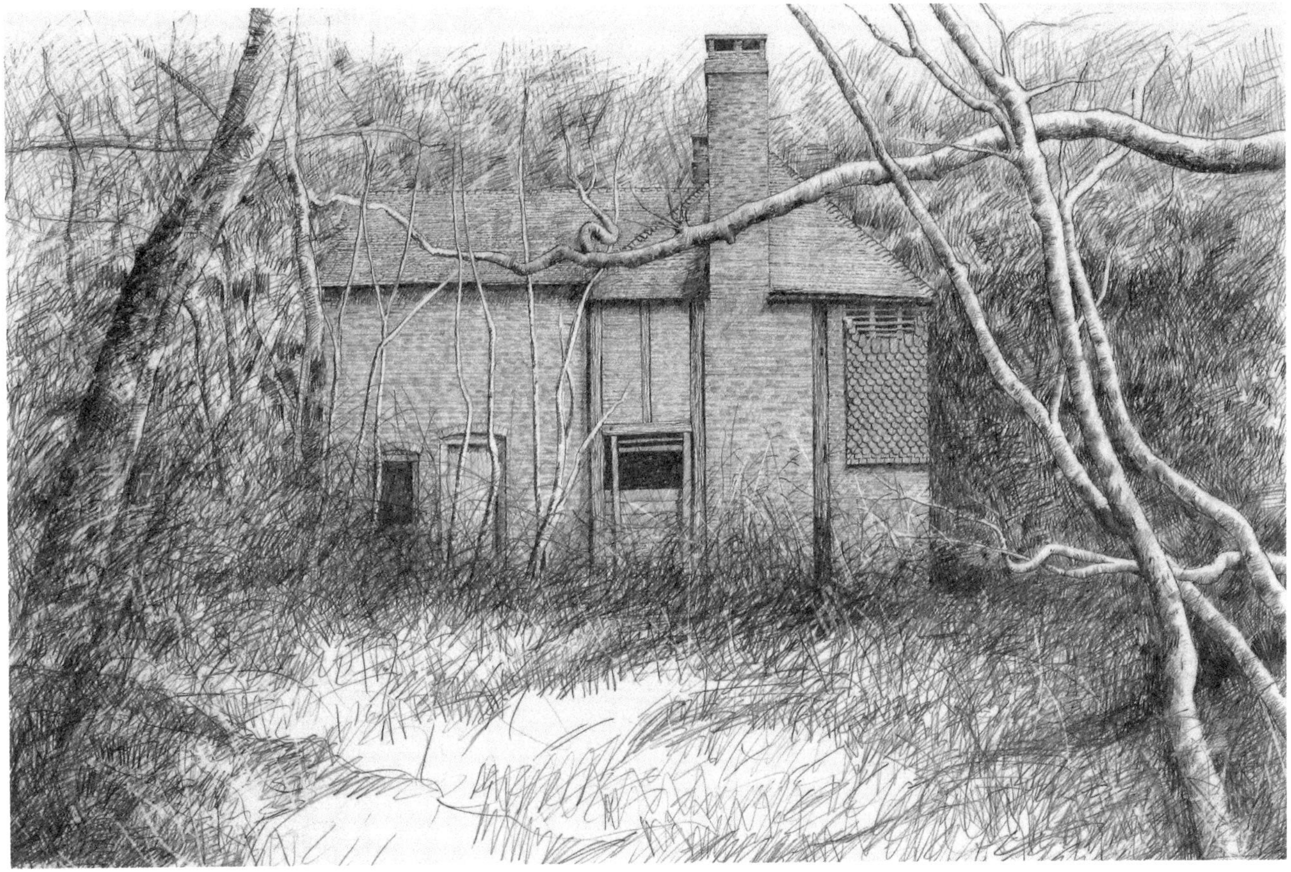

18

Stone shed near Lurgashall
21.0 × 42.0 cm.
(Private collection)

However humble, they were made by men who, as Flora Thompson said, deserve to be remembered for they knew the now lost secret of being happy on little. My drawings may constitute a record of something tangible but I need them also to celebrate those men who exist today only through the work they left behind.

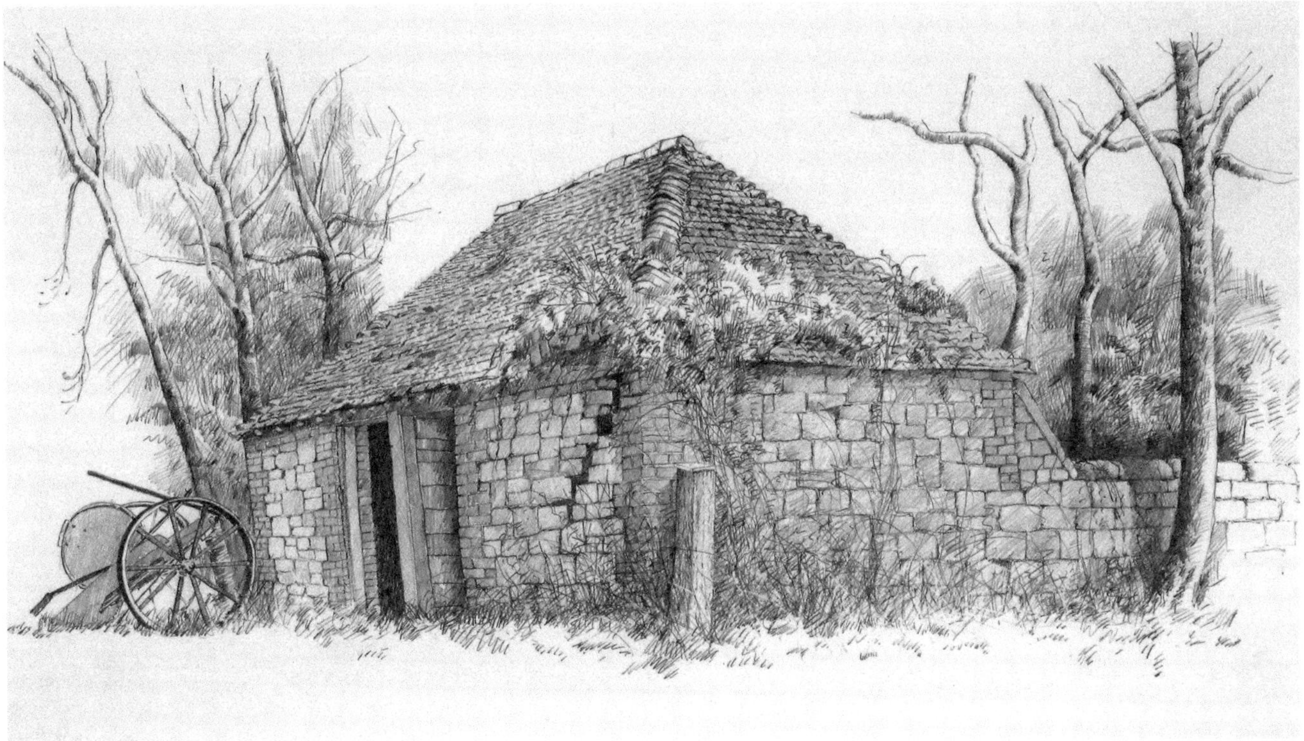

19

Derelict timber framed barn near Lurgashall (1)
29.0 × 35.4 cm.

FIRST VISIT

A Land-Rover rattles along the track, coiling and twisting the dry leaves that scamper behind it. Then it is all quiet again and a cock pheasant pecks without enthusiasm at some green shoots beside me as if I wasn't here.

SECOND VISIT

No Land-Rover, no pheasants, no barn. Just a tangle of beams and posts and tiles and a fragile skeleton and there is only so much you can reconstruct from memory. If these drawings have any point, then this is the one to prove it. A sense of sadness as if someone had died in the night while no-one was there.

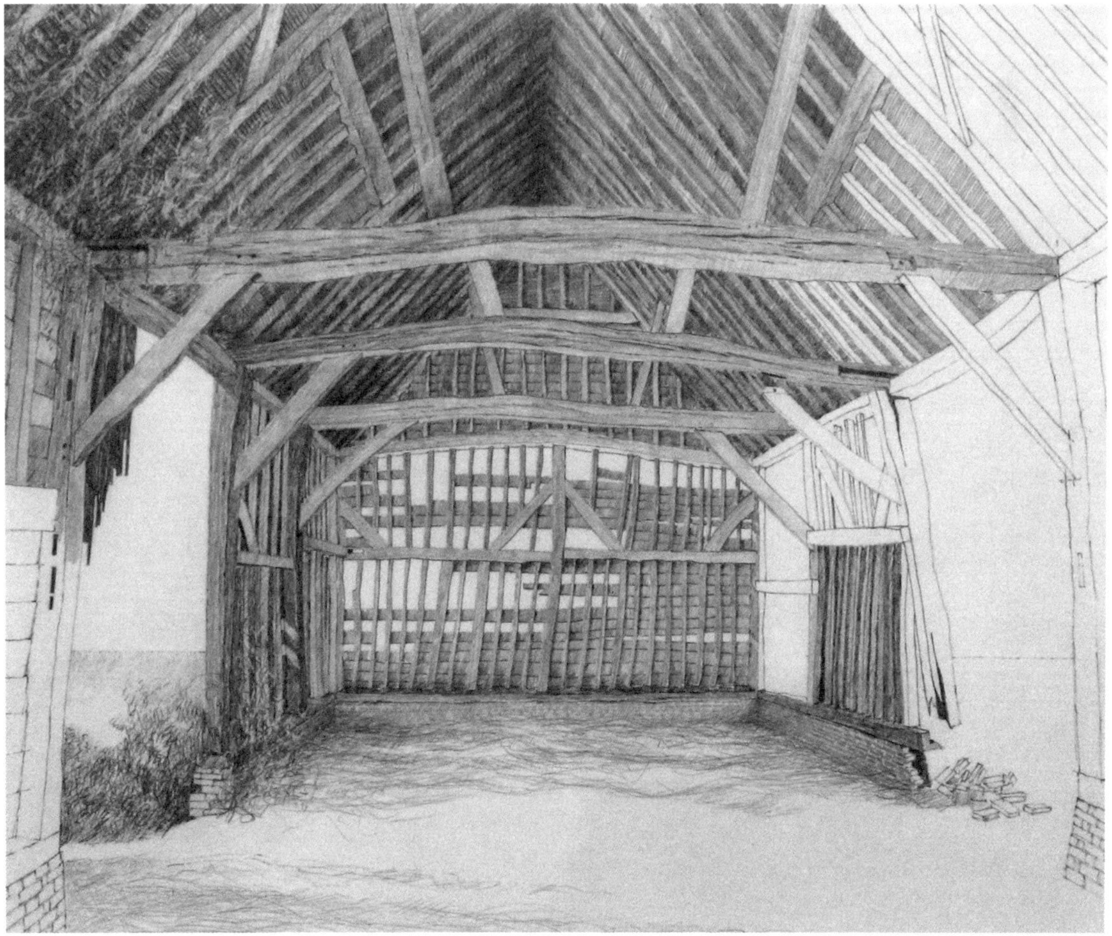

20

Derelict timber framed barn near Lurgashall (2)
27.5 × 40.5 cm.

"Do you work from photographs?" It's what they all ask. And I look at them and shake my head. Not for these drawings. Why make things more difficult for myself? It is hard enough working from life with the advantage of all the information there in front of me. However explicit the photograph it's only ever going to give you a fraction of that information. No, the only way is to be there and properly get to know and involve yourself with the subject. But I do take photographs – it's easier then to see which angle, which viewpoint, will make the better design.

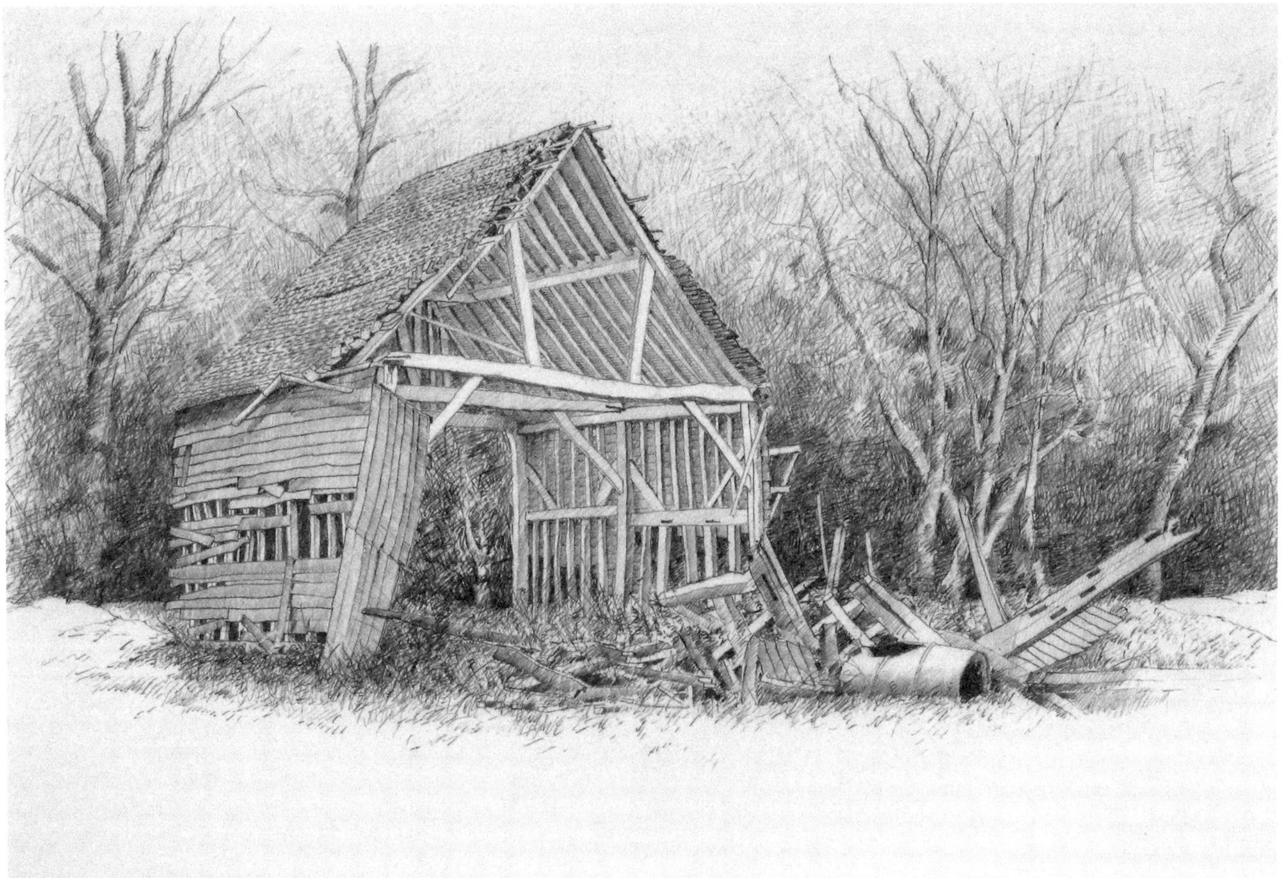

21

Derelict timber framed barn near Lurgashall (3)
25.6 × 36.3 cm.

There are no people in the drawings – and almost no animal life – cattle and high buzzards the rare exceptions. But there are the remains of people, traces of people. Wheel tracks in the snow, a ladder, a concrete mixer and bags of ballast waiting. The subjects, the barns, sheds and hovels are all about people. As they are extensions of the land on which they stand, they are equally extensions of the men who built them. Like the drawings these buildings were not planned – not in the way we excessively plan today, with committees and endless paperwork. No, they were needed, they were built, and once there, like unexpected features in a drawing, they will have assumed an inevitability.

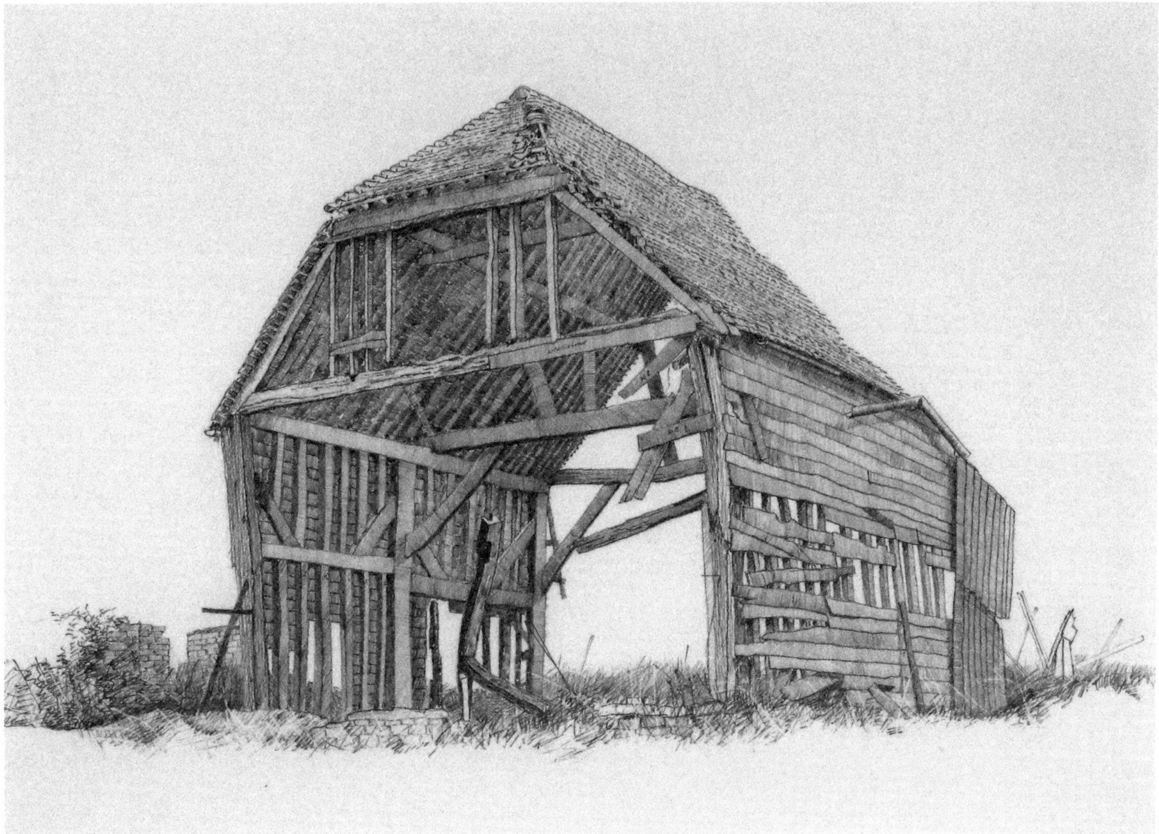

22

Dovecote at Stag Park
Farm, Petworth
29.3 × 44.0 cm.

I am not interested in pretty pastoral pictures. If these appear that way I don't think I've failed – it's just a sort of by-product, that's all. But I am quite interested in mystery. In this, the age of facts, when advertisers tell us that "... scientific tests have proved ..." and "... research shows that ...", we simply know too much. Or think we do. In all this certainty it is a function of art to create mystery. To ask questions and not to provide answers. To deal in ideas not knowledge. To take the known and re-describe it as the unknown.

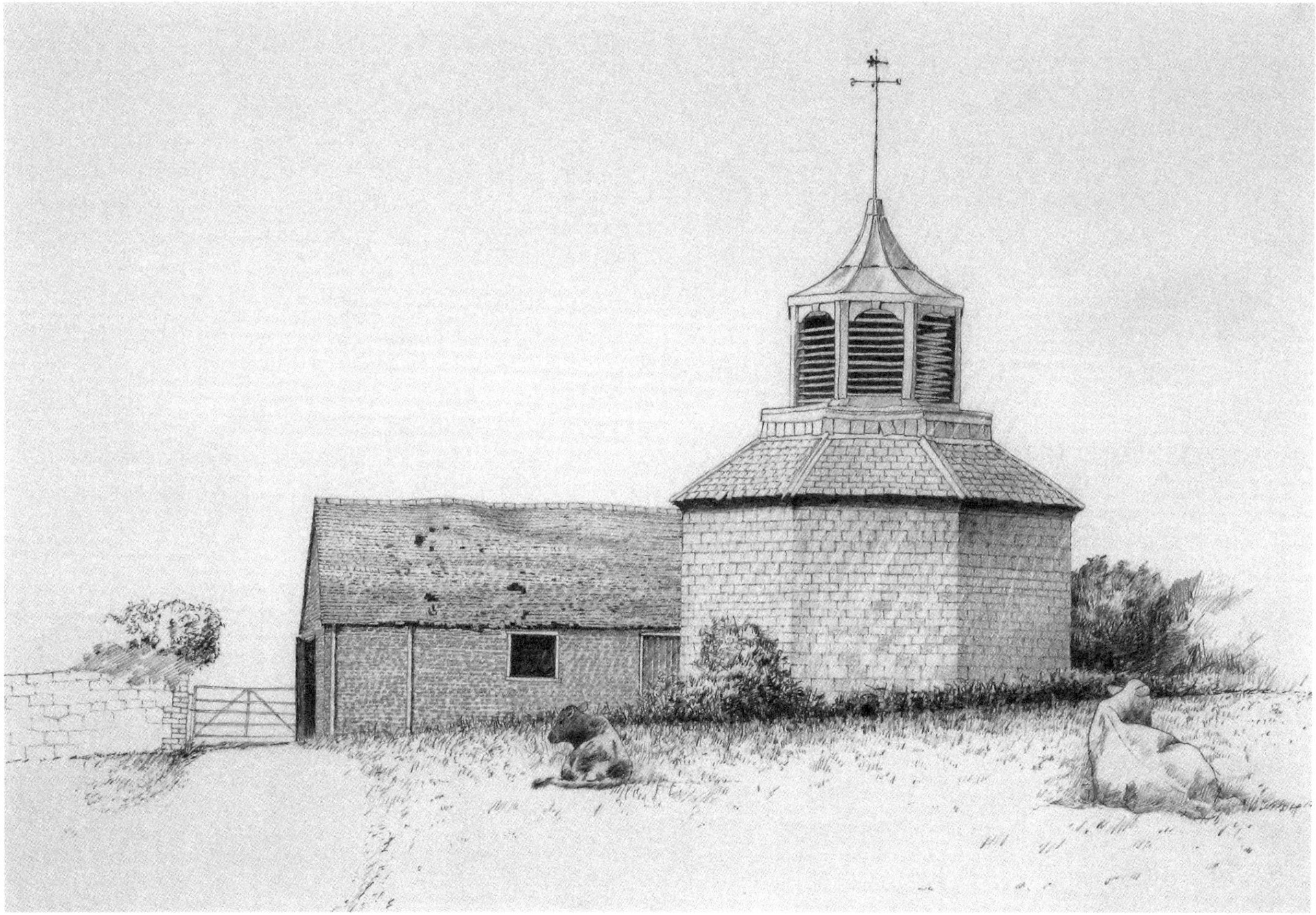

23

The Church of the Assumption of St Mary the Virgin, Church Farm Lane, East Wittering
27.0 × 37.2 cm.

The name of the church and its address sounded promising but Church Farm seems no longer to exist, replaced on one side by a small industrial estate of big pre-fabricated sheds called units. On the other a small estate of unaffordable affordable housing. Toytown architecture with dinky gables and pvc fittings. The Vauxhall Zafira on the tarmac drive because the detached garage (with sham cupola) will be stuffed with electric lawnmowers and wind-surfing tackle.

You can't get into the church. The little south door with its arch of chevrons is barred by scaffolding and galvanised mesh. There should be a lot of past here, a lot of history, but you can't feel it, apart from the headstones of course. There is one at the edge which has fallen into the ivy and last year's leaves and this year's snowdrops. Its pathetic and unashamed honesty is rare: "Sacred to the memory of Frederick J. Quick Aged 23 Years. Leading seaman, H.M.S. Narcissus who fell overboard from his ship and was drowned during the Review of the Fleet off the Isle of Wight by H.I.M. the German Emperor on August 6th, 1889." You don't know whether to laugh or cry. Actually I do. I'm not laughing.

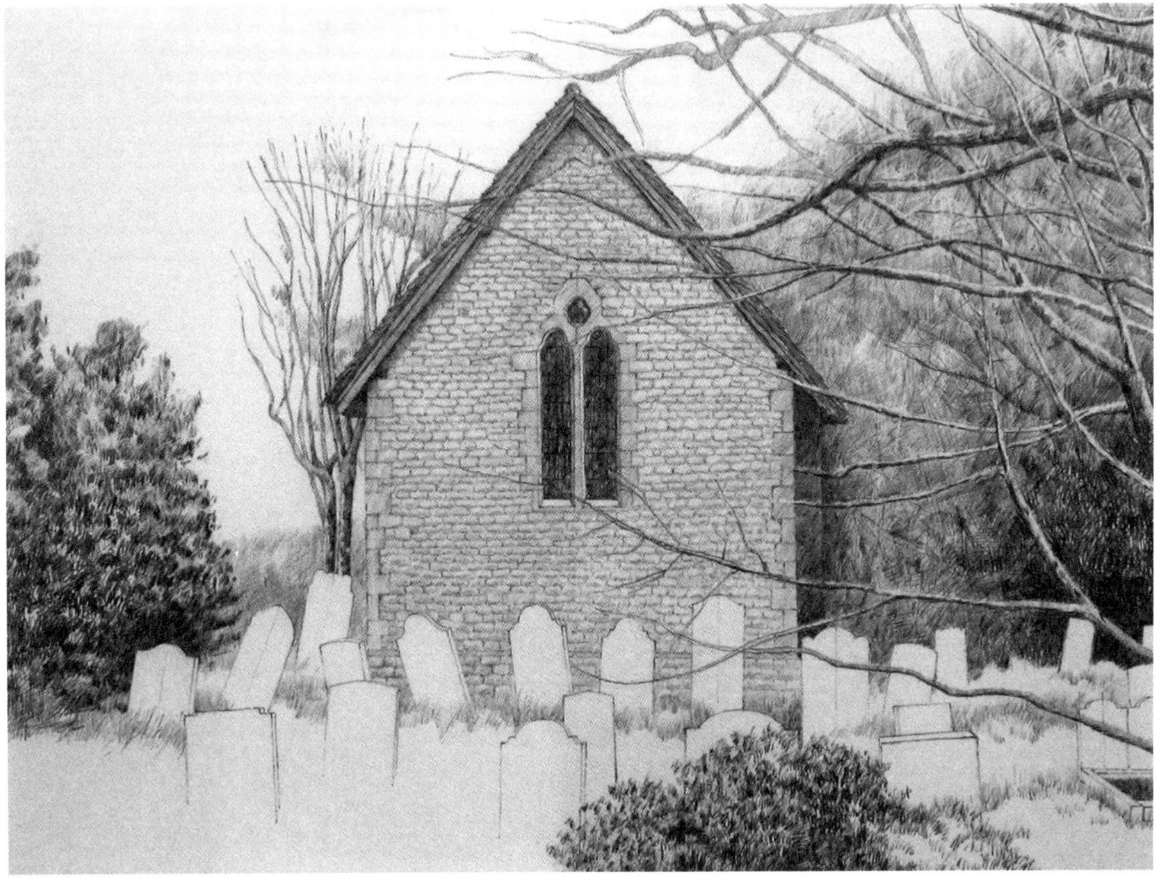

24

Roadside barn at
Strood Farm, Byworth
28.8 × 46.4 cm.

The lure of the unfinished persists. *The Mystery of Edwin Drood* is not Dickens' best but it might be the most interesting. Ask anyone to name a Schubert symphony and the chances are it will be the one he didn't finish. An uncompleted sentence gives the listener a chance to be creative. But it's so difficult to stop a drawing. Perhaps there should be a time limit, like in an exam.

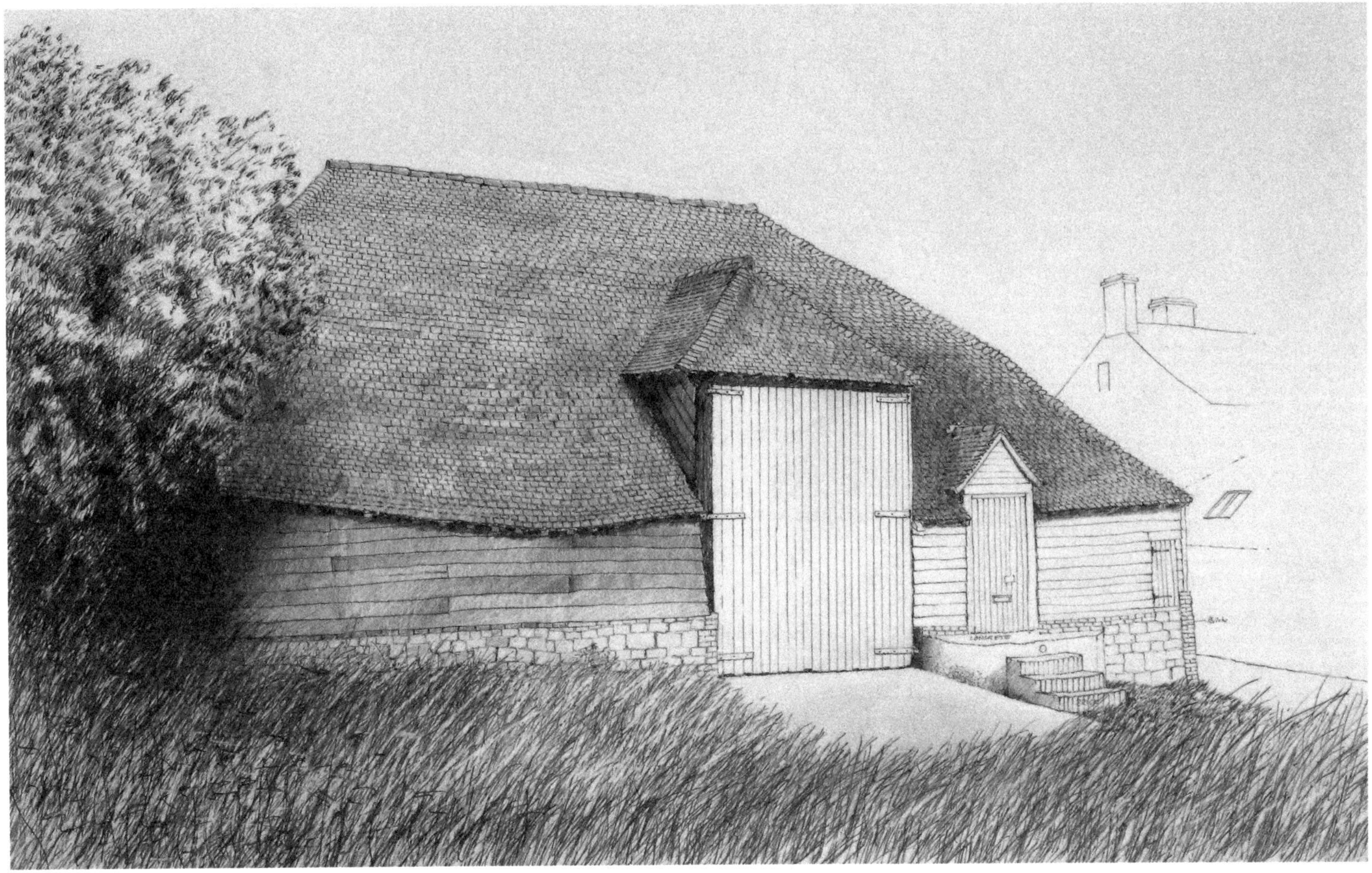

25

Field barn near Egdean
29.8 × 40.5 cm.

It's not old. Perhaps a hundred and fifty years but now forgotten in a wide field of clover.

A low Chinook, its six blades thumping the air, too slowly it would seem, to hold its lead-grey mass in the thin air. These low-flying exercises a preparation for Afghanistan. Do I sit here among clover or are these poppies? *Papaver somniferum.* Nitrogen or opium? IEDs on the bridleway back through the wood.

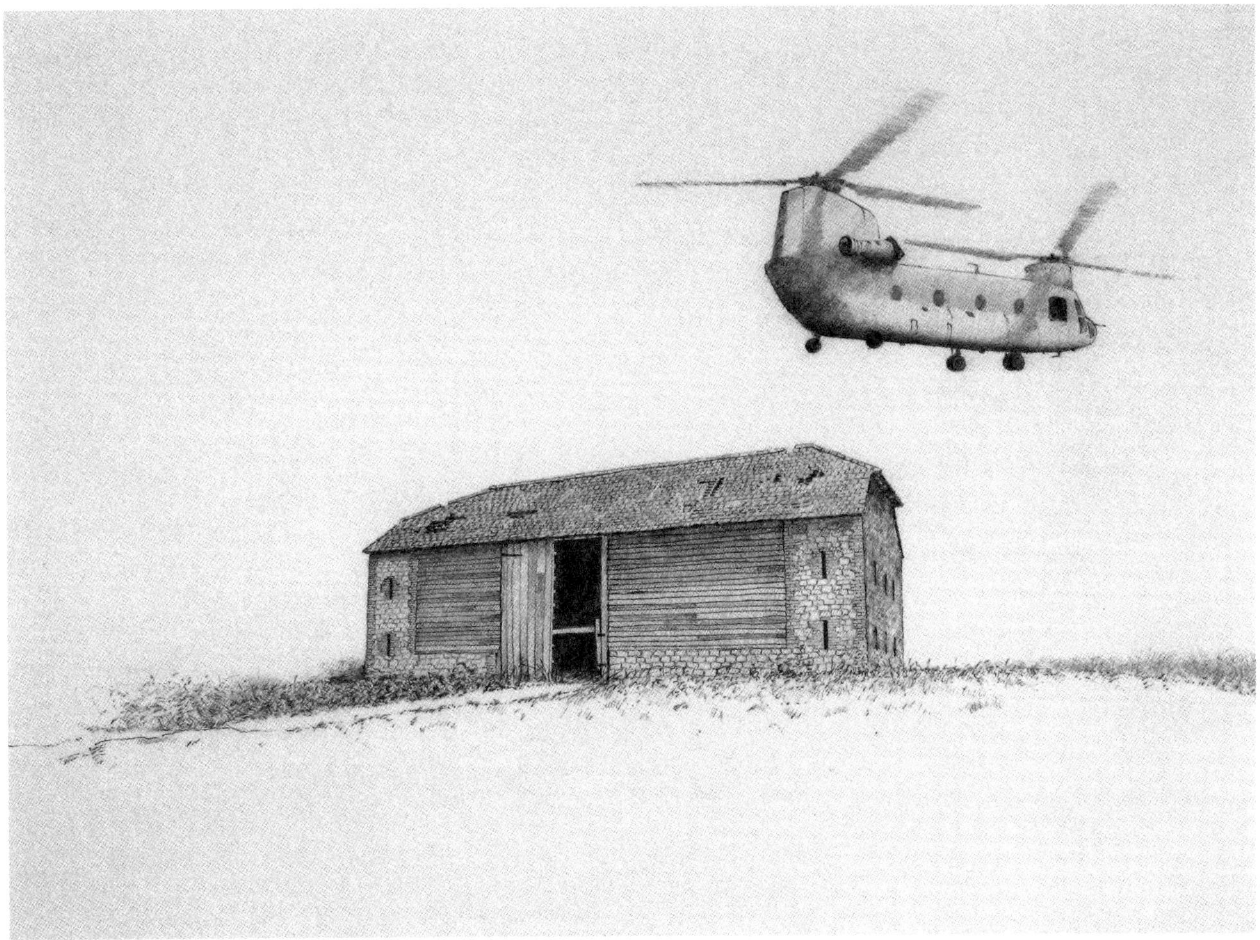

26

Field barn and stock-
yard near Egdean
23.5 × 33.5 cm.

Nettles and docks, brambles and goose-grass. Elders drooping and heavy with fruit which is neither black nor blue nor red but all of these. Metallic flies, green and blue, jerk over the brittle pellets and the grey-white guano below the barn owl's box.

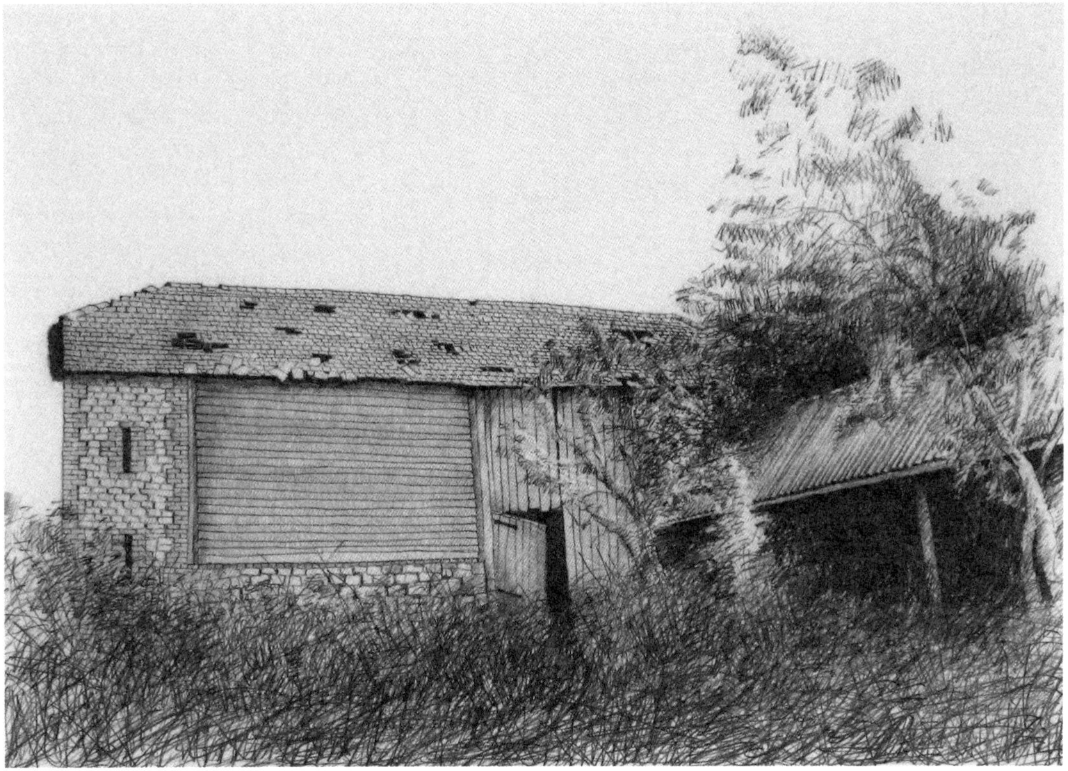

27

Hallgate Farm,
Byworth (1)
26.0 × 41.8 cm.

A passing car and a fragment of a tune that seems strangely inappropriate. "There's a hole in Daddy's arm where all the money goes / And Jesus Christ died for nothing, I suppose."

Inappropriate? John Prine's anti-war song would seem so in this concrete summer yard with the hollyhocks over there and the sounds of chickens from the other side. Yet it was not that long ago that a low-flying helicopter rattled the slates of the field barn I was drawing. The world is a much smaller place than when these buildings were made and although we argue and bicker over details we are all, whatever we think as idealists or pragmatists, in the same boat. There's a waterfall ahead and we're looking for an overhanging branch to cling to.

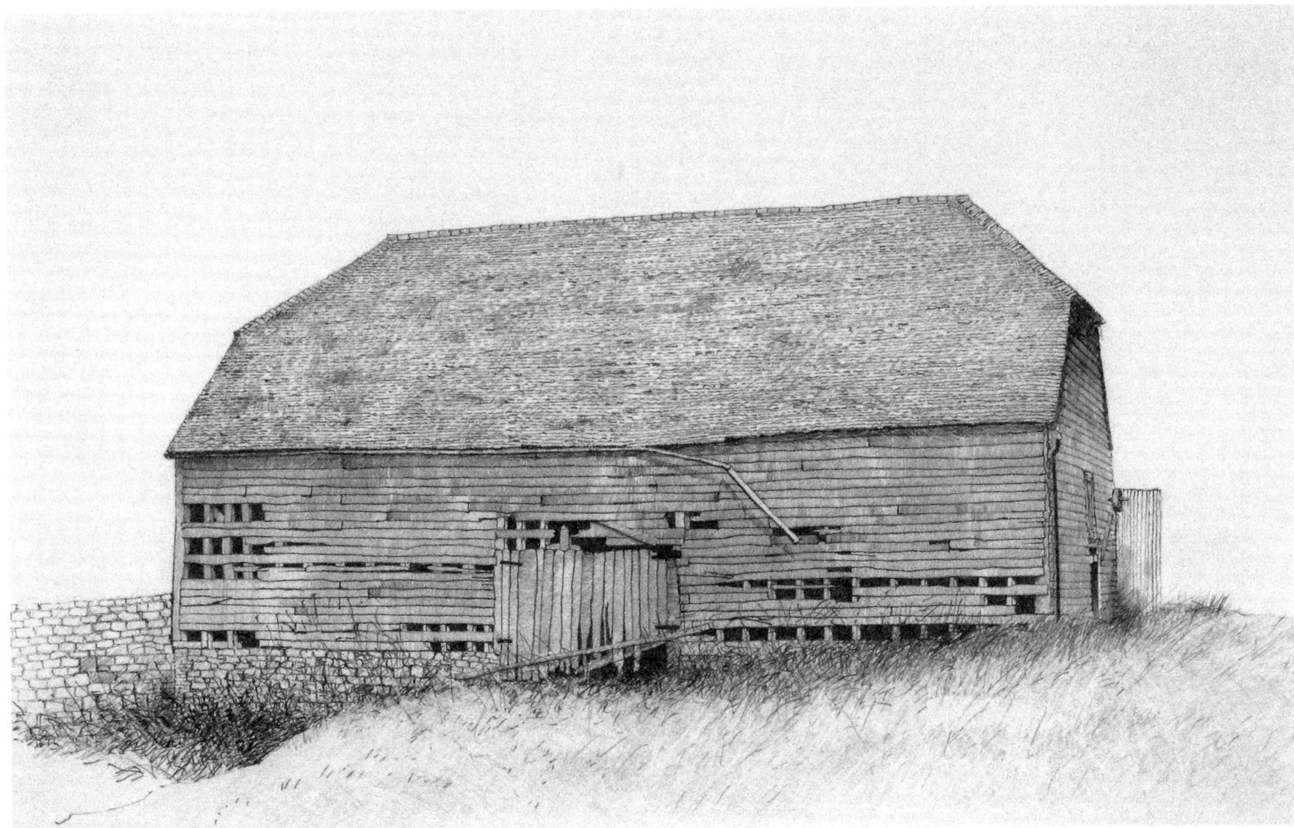

28

Hallgate Farm,
Byworth (2)
26.0 × 40.0 cm.

I feel to be something of a descendant of those contributors to 'Recording Britain' all those years ago. It seems their work is never far from me – Badmin's precision (he always reminds me of Thomas the Tank Engine) or Walter Bayes' Ardizzone-like scribbles. But these buildings are not threatened by enemy action or even, with the odd exception, by developers' schemes. Threatened though by time and change, as everything is and as we all are.

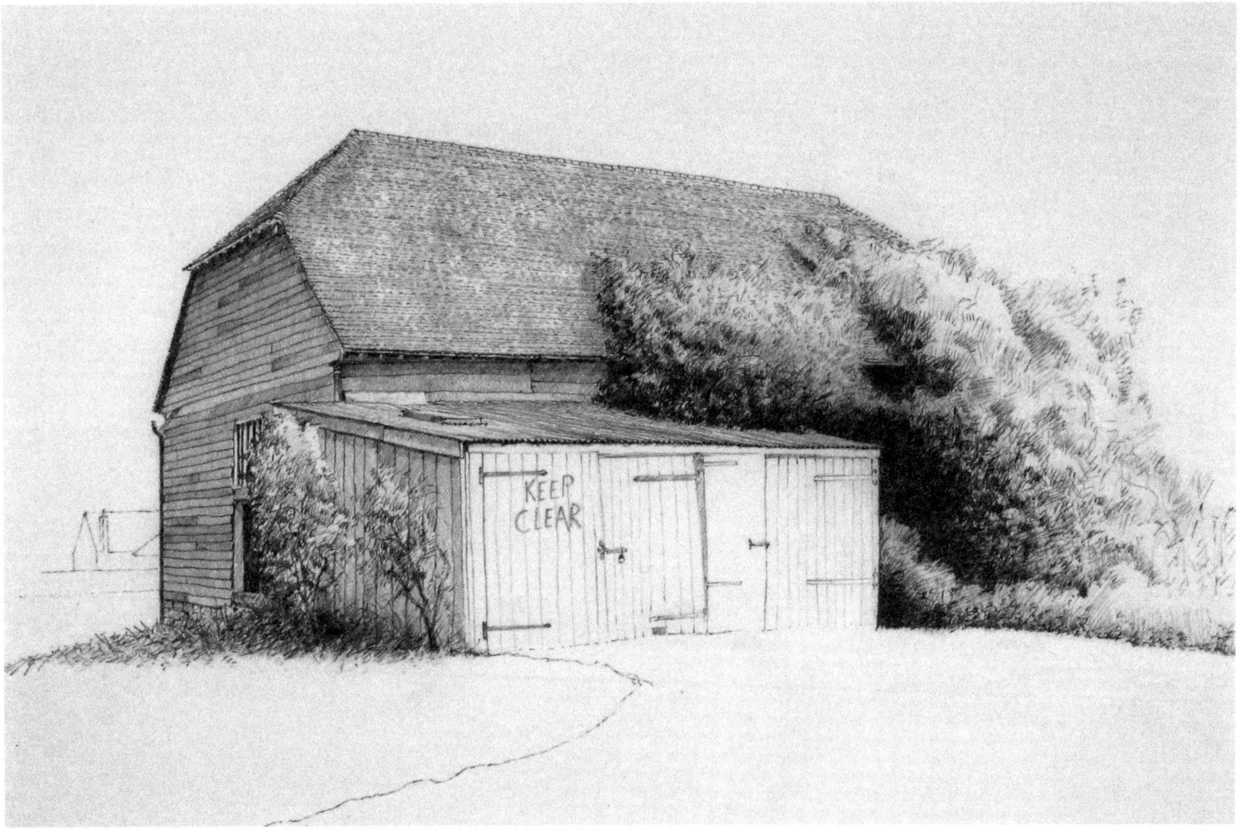
KEEP
CLEAR

29

Hallgate Farm,
Byworth (3)
31.0 × 41.0 cm.
(Private collection)

Christmas. It's a sort of pregnancy (which it is). It starts in March or April but only the marketing departments know of it. By June and July the fashion editors and stylists are with the photographers and by October it's become public. The shop windows are the first to tell the story and by December I am sick of it.

But here in this hay-strewn barn that's stood for a very long time, you can, with a tiny belief that overcomes all the hype, imagine that there really was, long ago, a baby born in a stable.

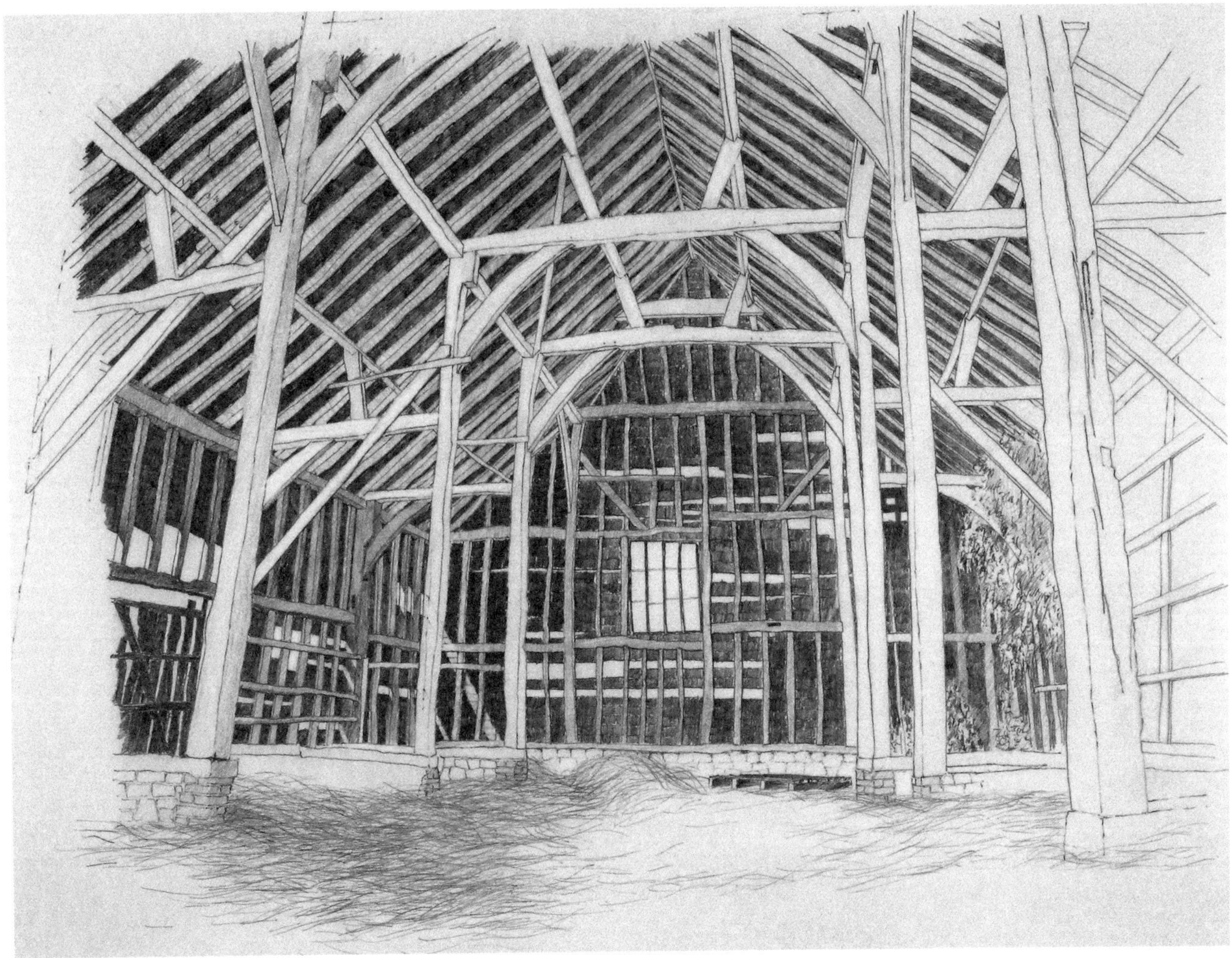

30

Field barn in the snow
near Petworth (1)
27.6 × 45.0 cm.

I enjoy the idea of the empty landscape where nothing happens. Where the nothing is emphatic and it makes you think of what it is that is not happening. It's more difficult than considering what is happening but it's frequently more rewarding.

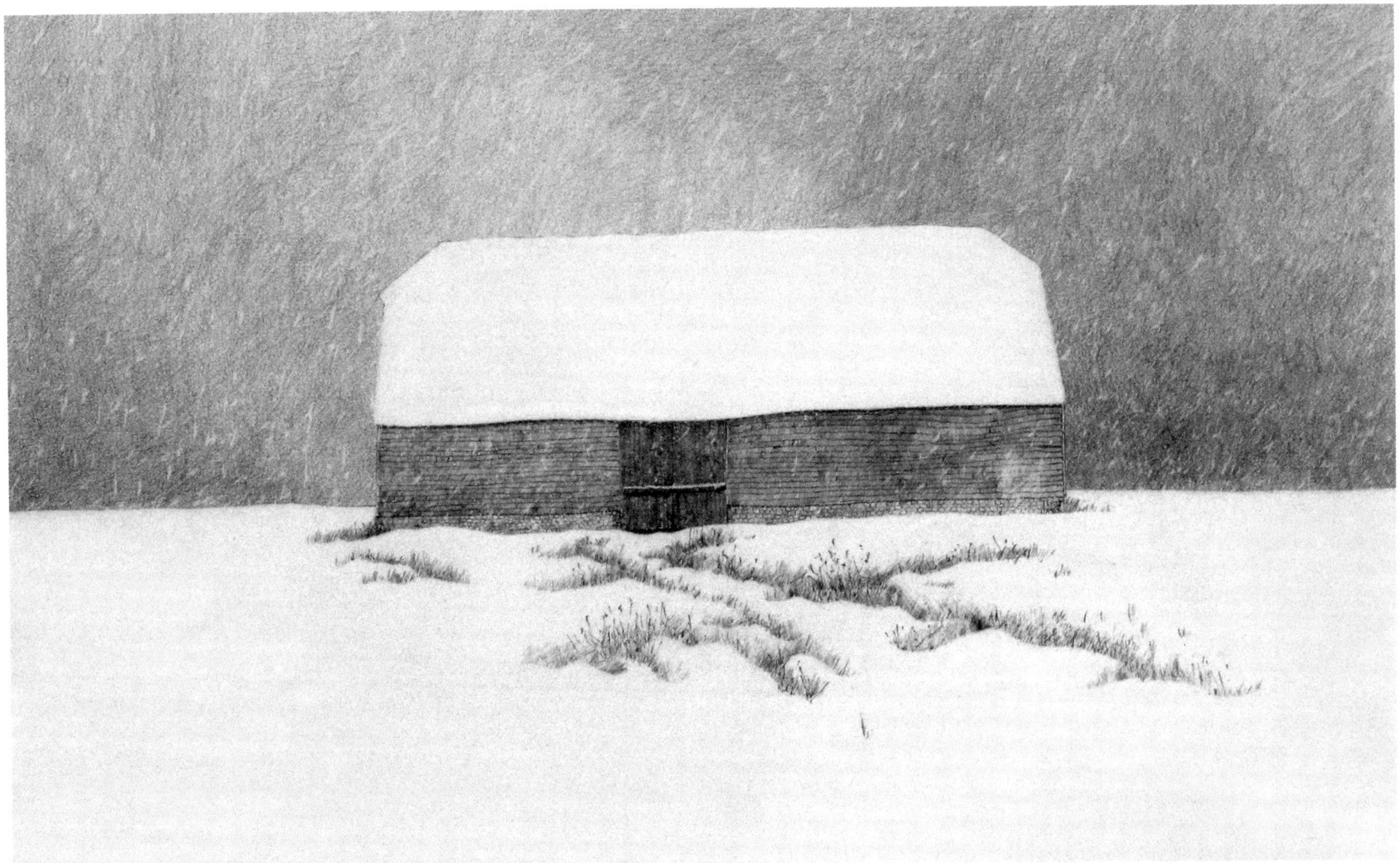

31

Field barn in the snow
near Petworth (2)
32.0 × 43.0 cm.
(Private collection)

Cold. Very, very cold.

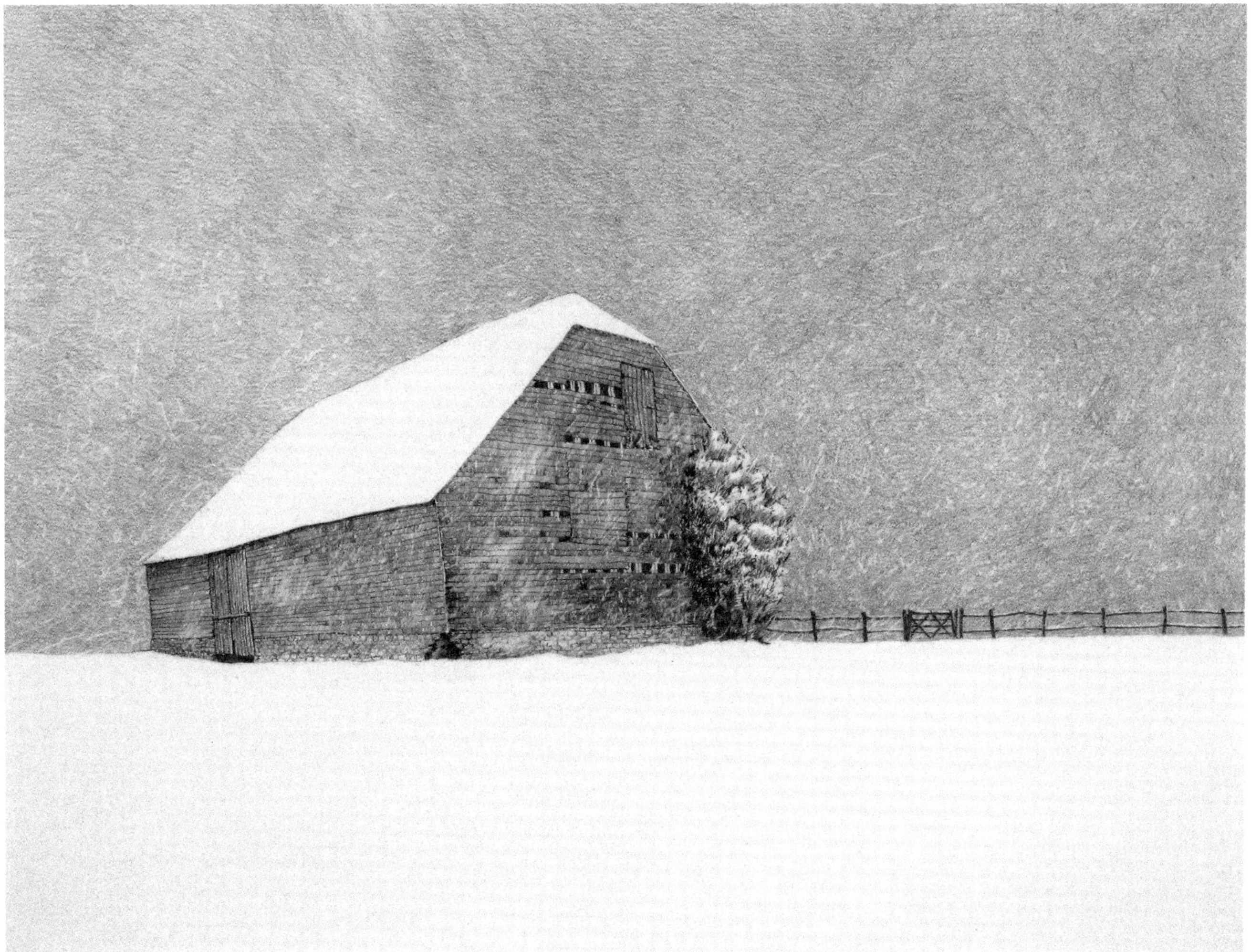

32

Stone and timber farm buildings near Byworth (1)
29.0 × 34.0 cm.
(Private collection)

I'm not happy here and I don't really want to make this drawing. It's not the cold, it's not the damp. It's the lack of love. As lovers who fall out of favour and into disuse, so farm buildings, once loved tend to reveal an old sense of being loved, of being made with love. Not here. As it isn't the cold and damp, neither is it the detritus of contemporary farm workers from far away – the lager cans, the crisp packets, the agricultural junk. And the turds (are there really dogs as big as this?) but these don't help.

Yet there is something. You don't see it at first and it's not much – just a radiused quoin in stone. Why was it done?

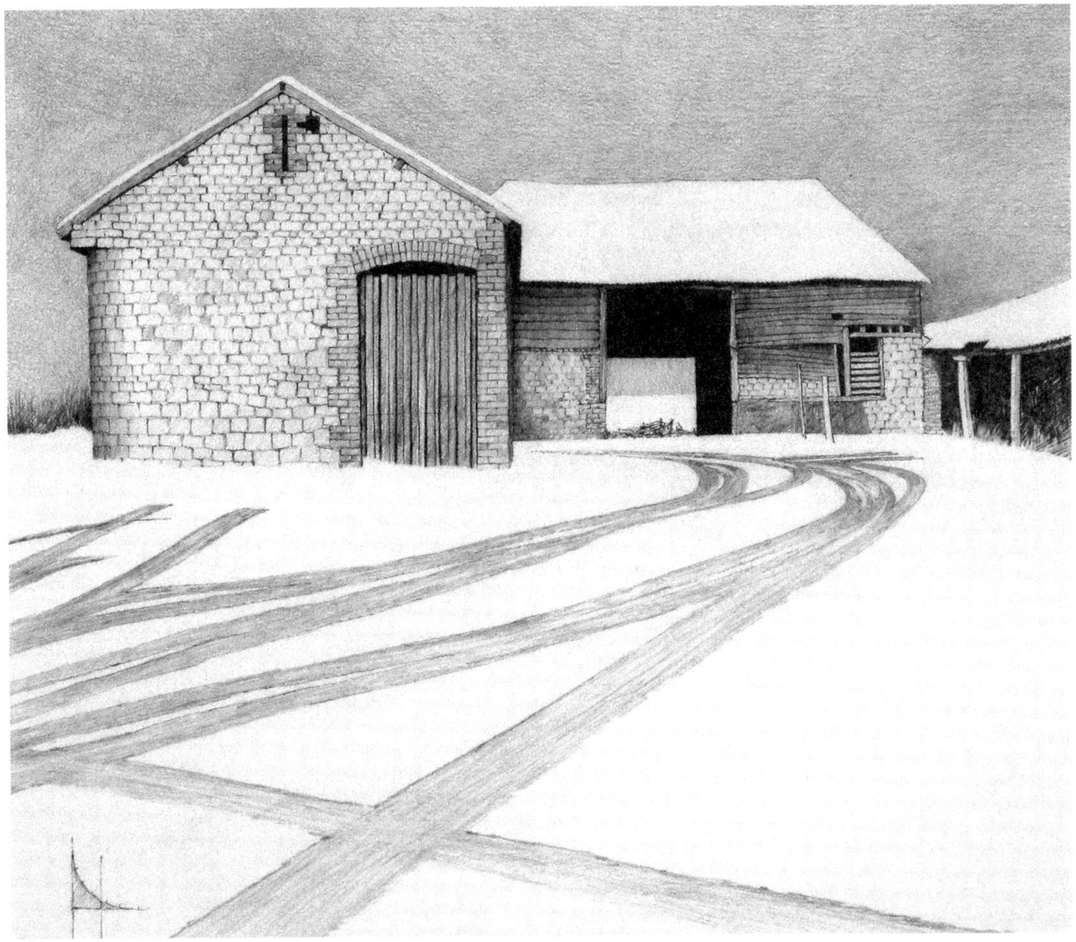

33

Stone and timber farm buildings near Byworth (2)
25.2 × 35.0 cm.

There is some repetition, of course there is. Thoughts and ideas which seem at the time to be specific to one location are inevitably subject to being apposite to others. Equally, there may be contradictions.

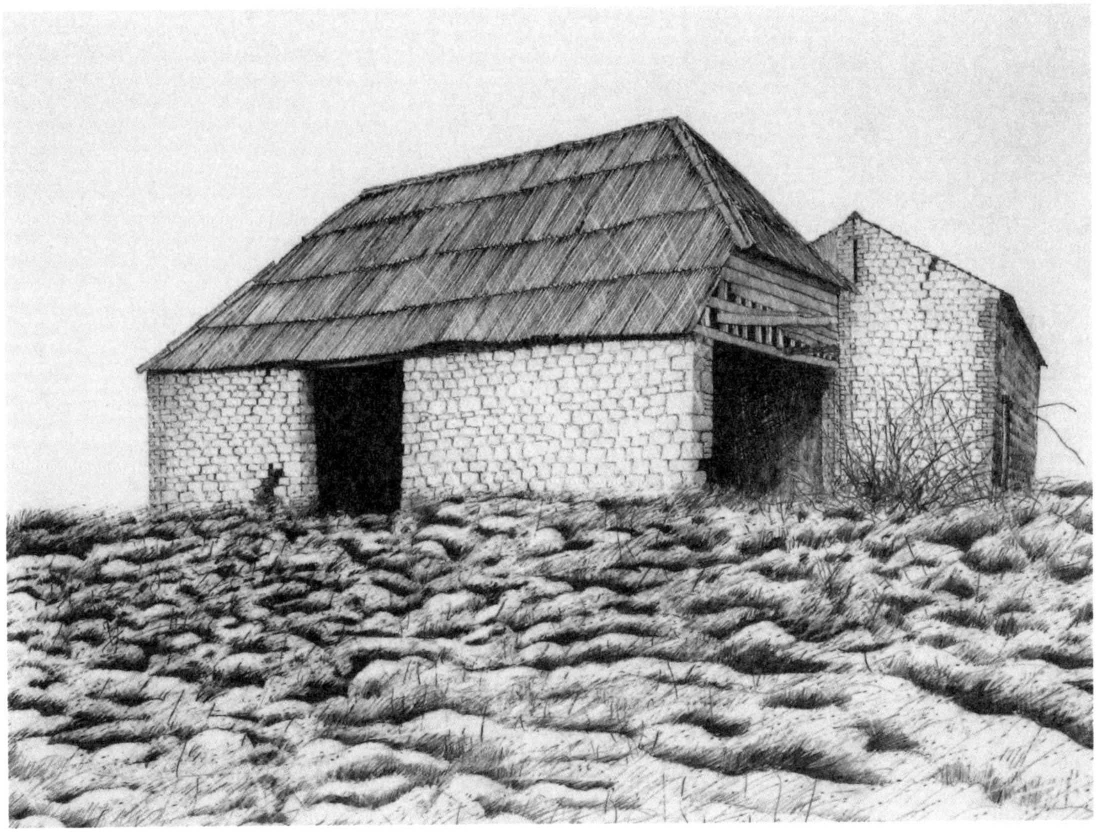

34

Timber framed barn near Petworth (1)
27.0 × 45.0 cm.
(Private collection)

I like the things I'm not supposed to like. I like, in a picture, the things I don't like in life – broken wire from a rusting staple in a wooden post, a lump of concrete and especially things which are linear. A fence, a line of telegraph poles (preferably with some leaning a bit). Even, in the distance, a row of pylons.

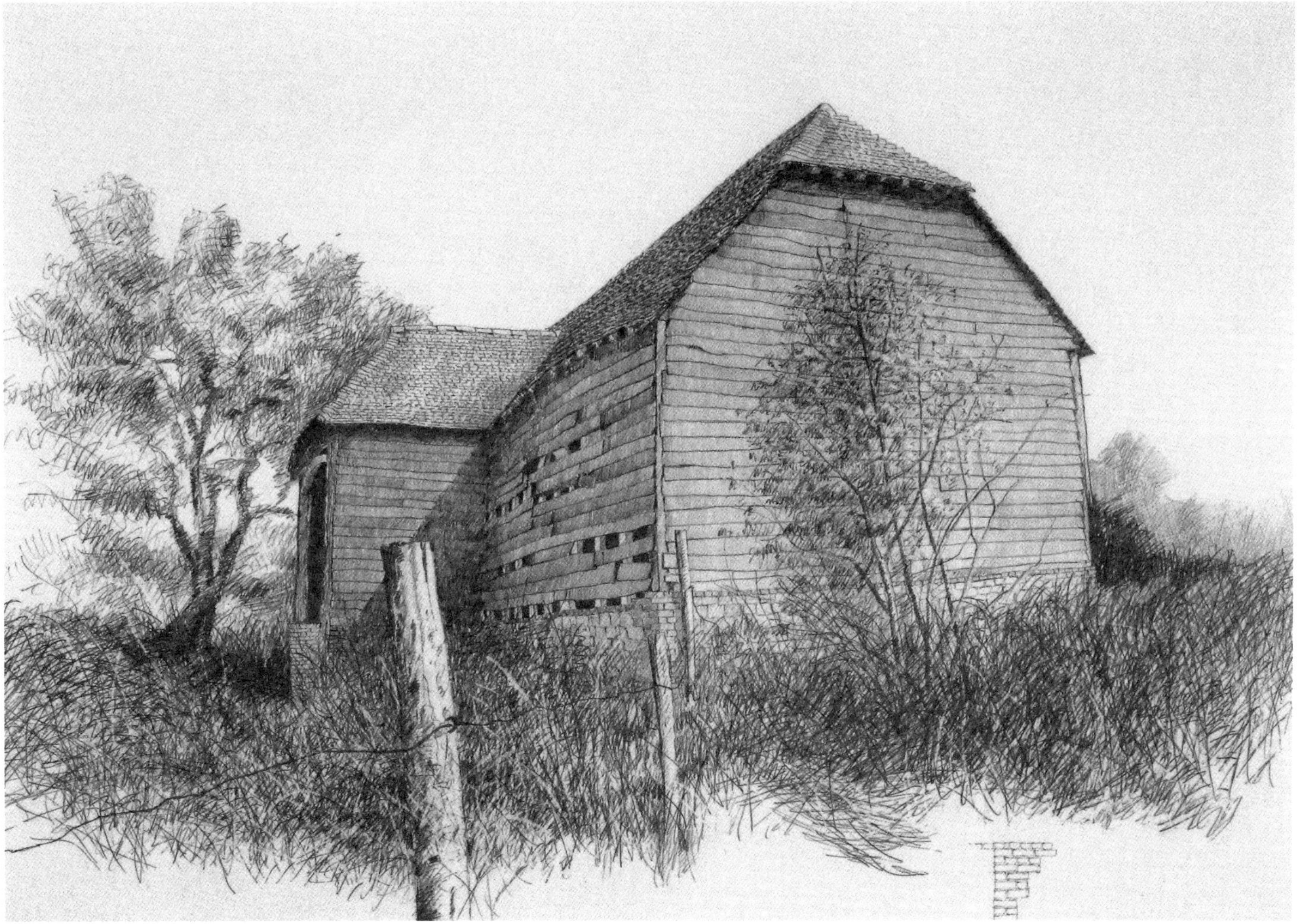

35
Timber framed barn
near Petworth (2)
25.8 × 41.8 cm.

Apart from using the camera to establish viewpoints and proportion there's no rehearsal. It's on to the paper and get it right first time – or wrong. And put up with it. But of course it's never right – and if it were it would be wrong.

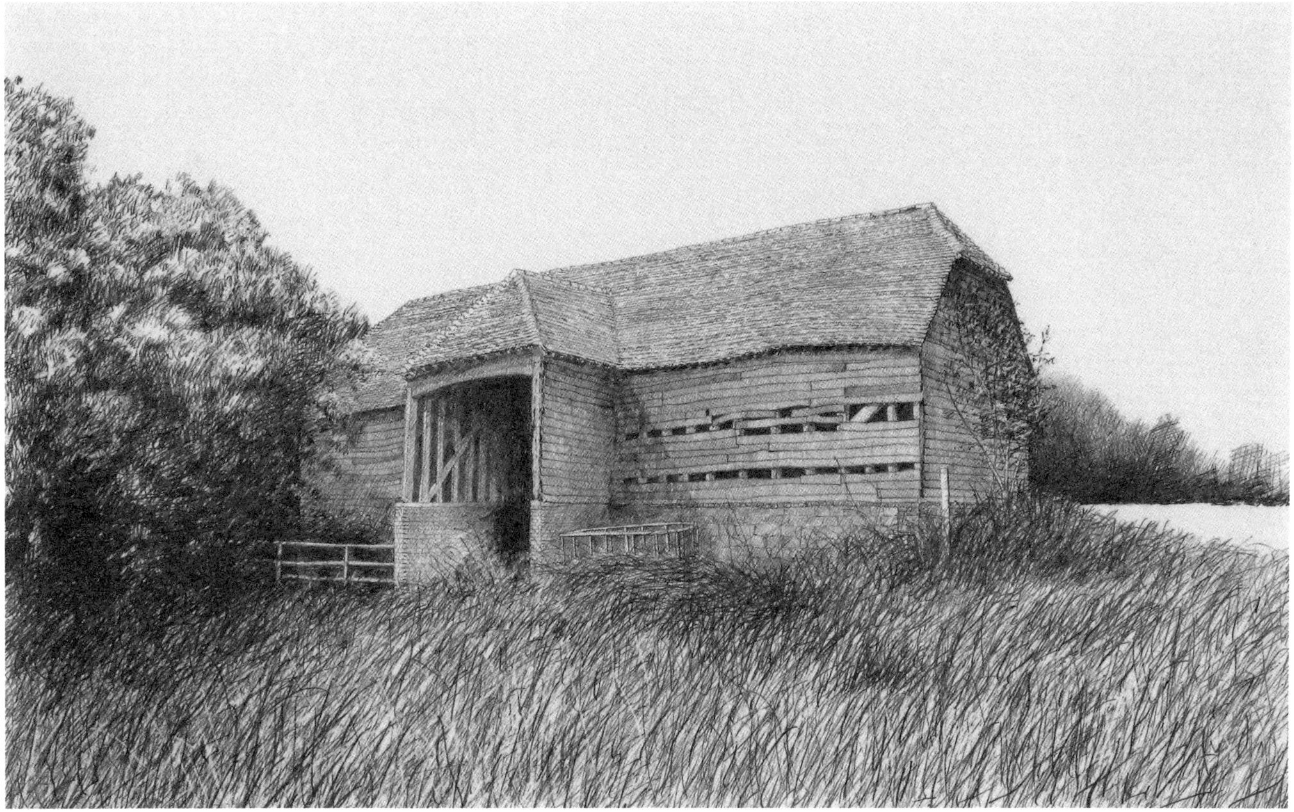

36

Frog Farm,
Petworth (1)
26.3 × 40.0 cm.

Buzzards circling on thermals. Low at first but soon so high they leave nothing but their calls. Like lost kittens. The corrugated silo clicks its expansion in the morning sun.

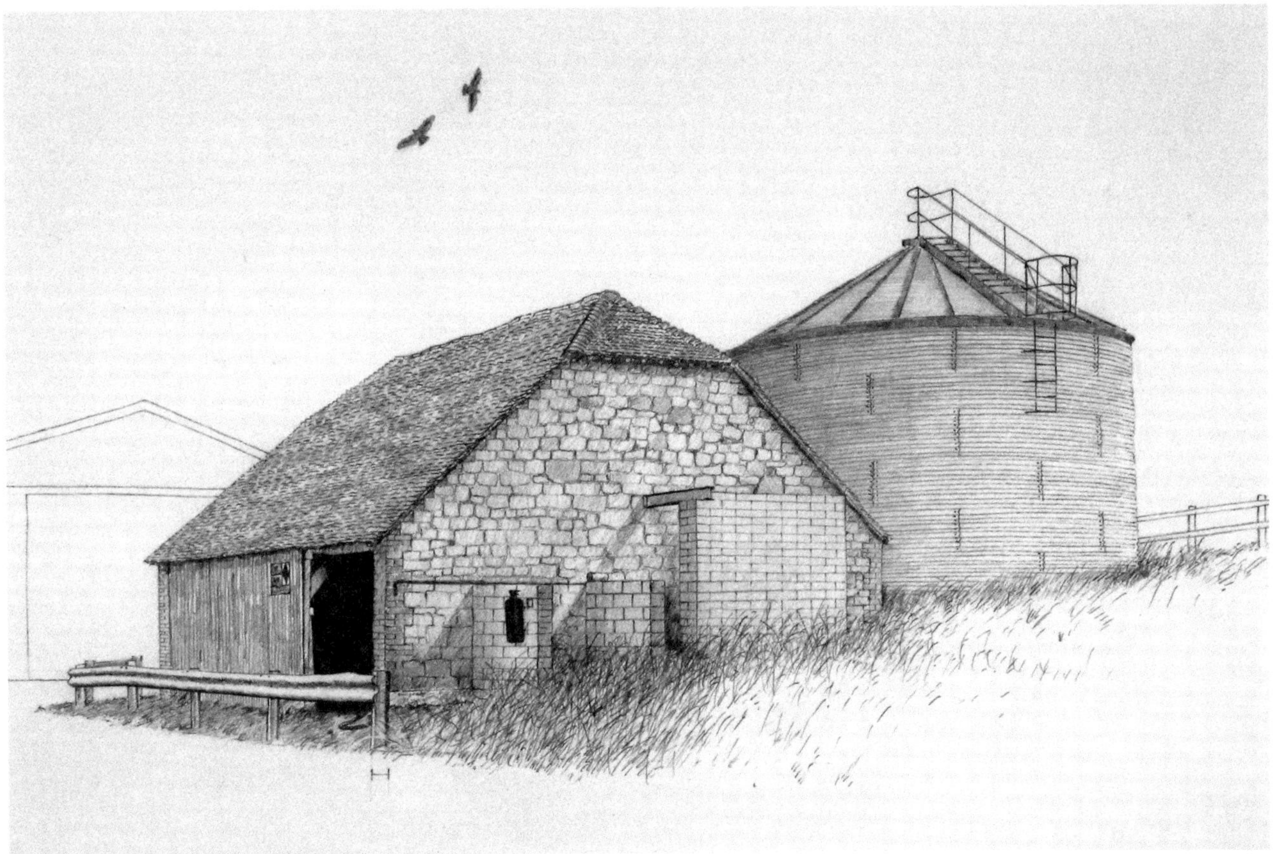

37

Frog Farm,
Petworth (2)
27.6 × 40.8 cm.

Cries from the football field beyond the main road. A loose door bangs although there's barely a breeze and the drizzle drifts aimlessly. This feels like the far perimeter of a little-used military airfield. You'd find Nissen huts long past their use, mossy and leaking. Things once purposeful, loved even, now sink year by year into the sandy ground. Perfume of spilled diesel.

The referee's whistle alerts me to the present and a white Transit splashes past. The faces at the wet windows the faces of farm workers from eastern Europe, yet here they tell of prisoners of war, gaunt, hungry for freedom.

Is that someone's coat, wet, heavy and half hidden?

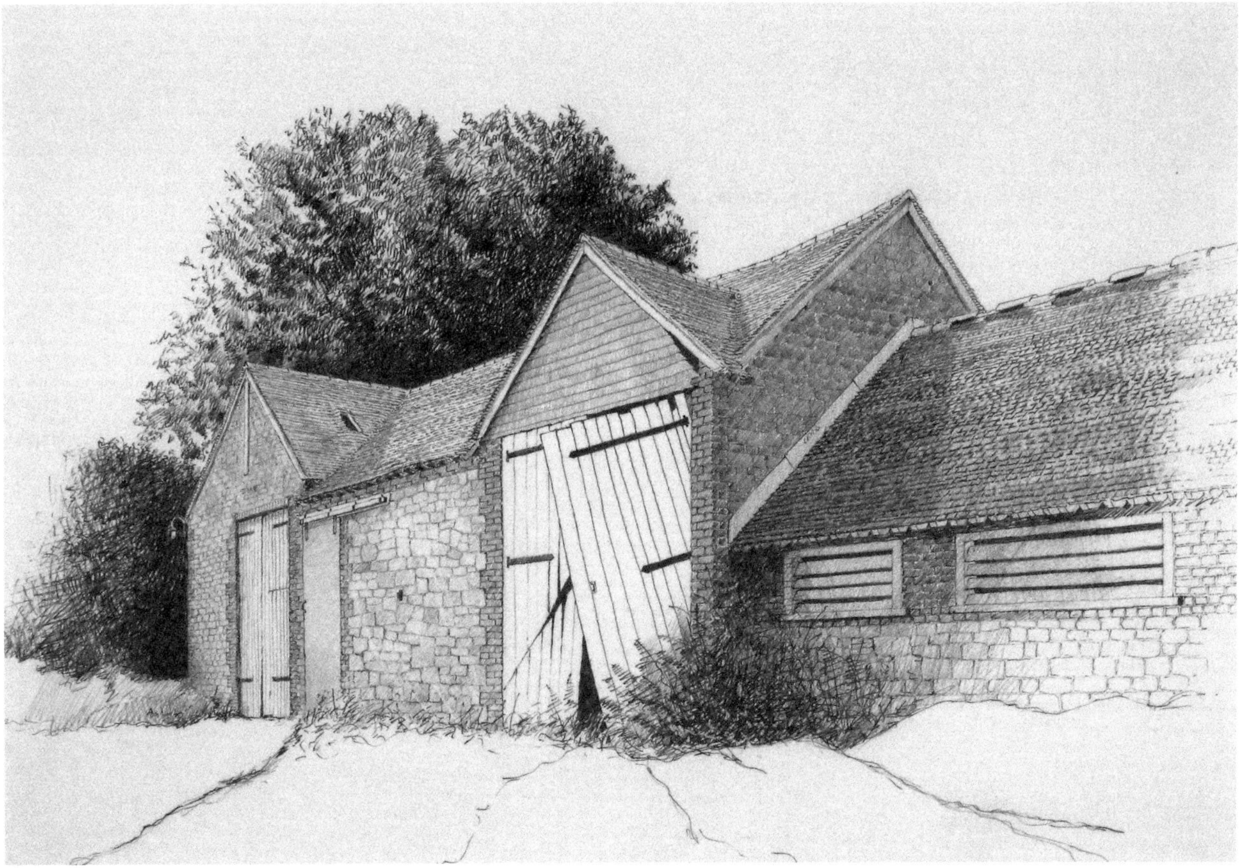

38

Stone barn at Coxlands Farm, Petworth
29.5 × 43.1 cm.

Tractors waiting on the far side. Orange lights flashing with an insistent rhythm not unlike a fast heartbeat. This is farming on a different scale – this is not farming, this is a campaign. The world is hungry. But there is none so hungry as the farmer's bank account.

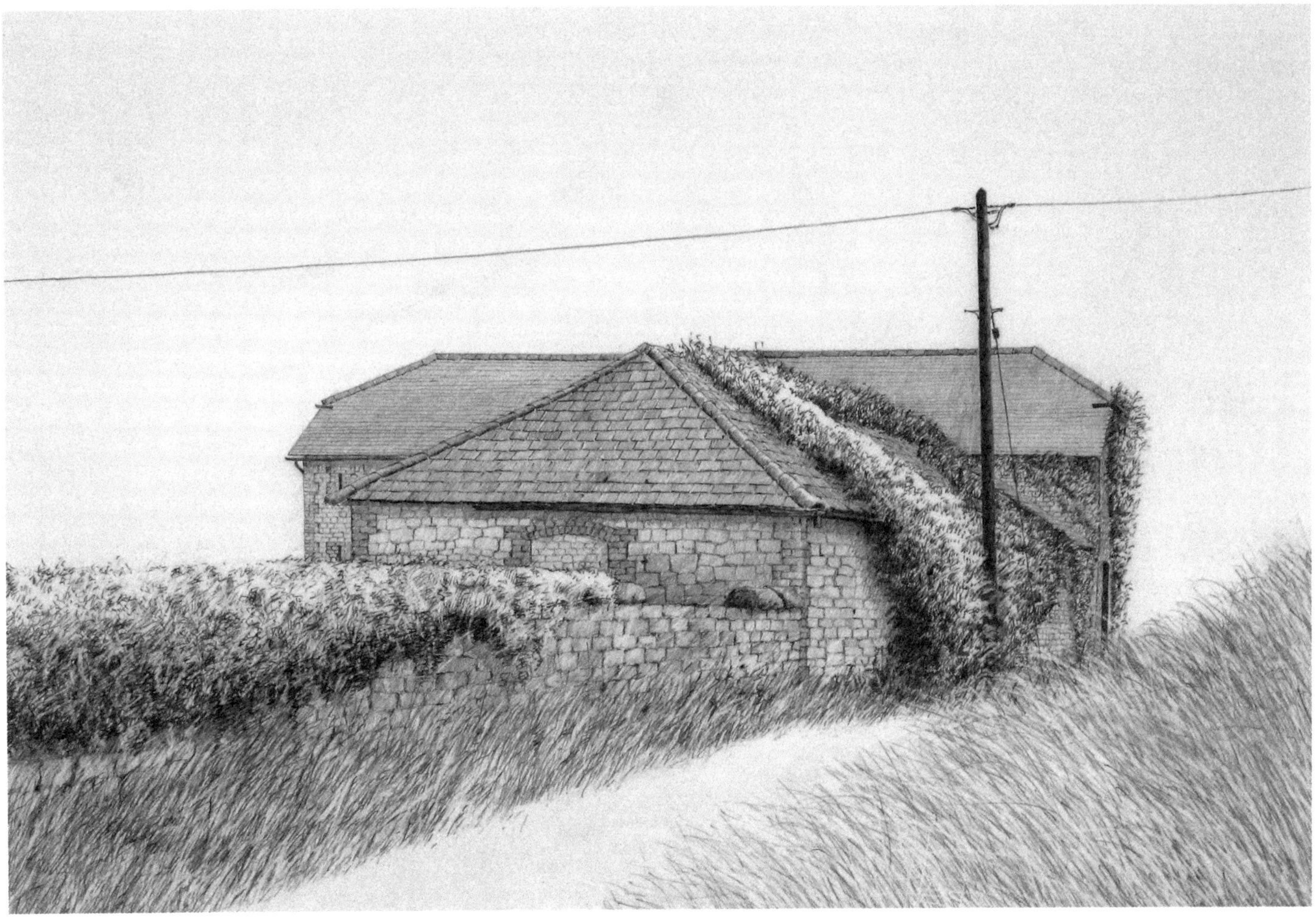

39

Sokenholes Farmhouse,
Petworth
31.6 × 40.0 cm.

Sometimes there is nothing to say and you hope the drawing will find something to say for you.

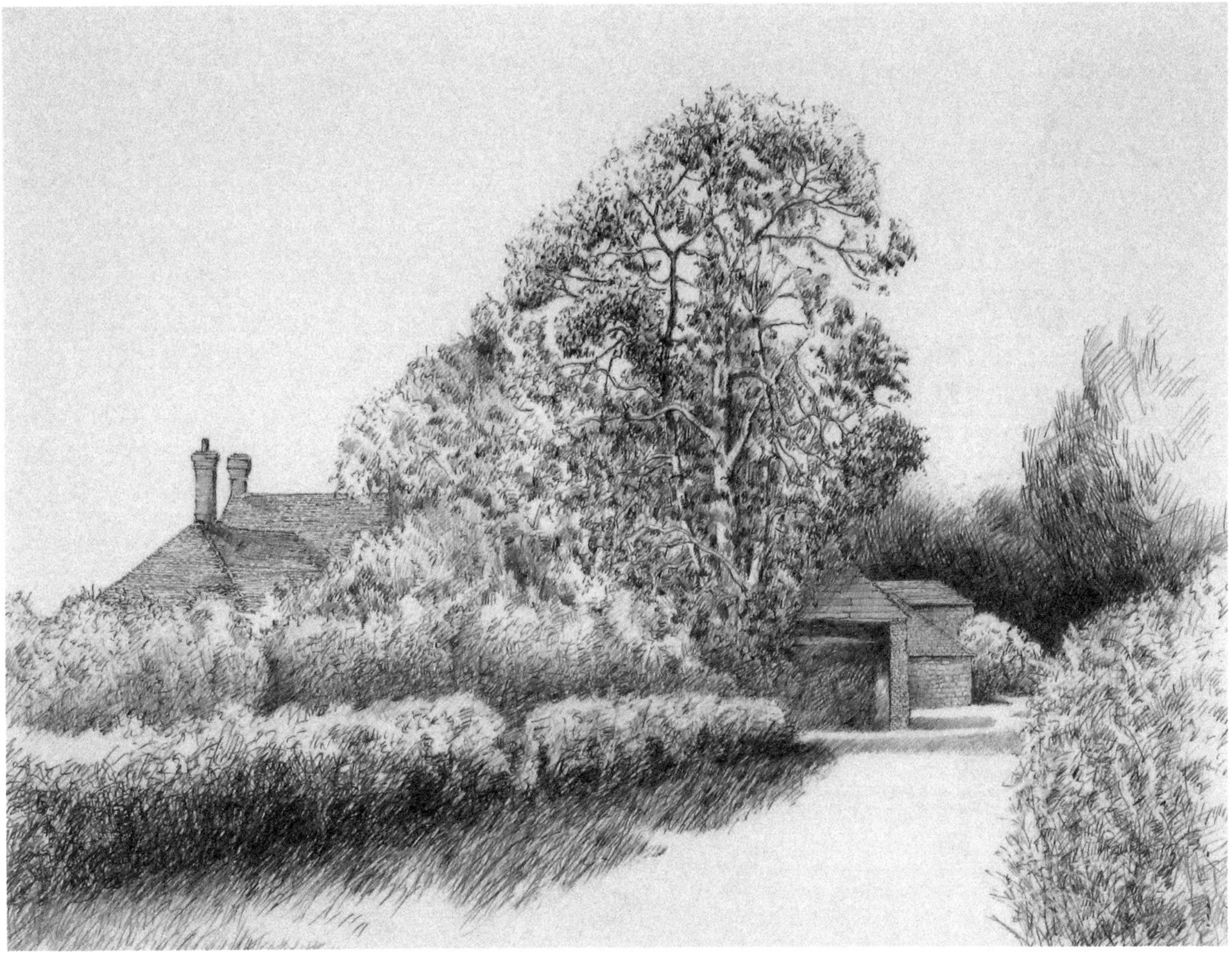

40

Outbuilding at
Sokenholes Farm,
Petworth
31.6 × 40.0 cm.

"If only these walls could talk," they say. Well, they do talk, are talking. But you have to learn how to listen.

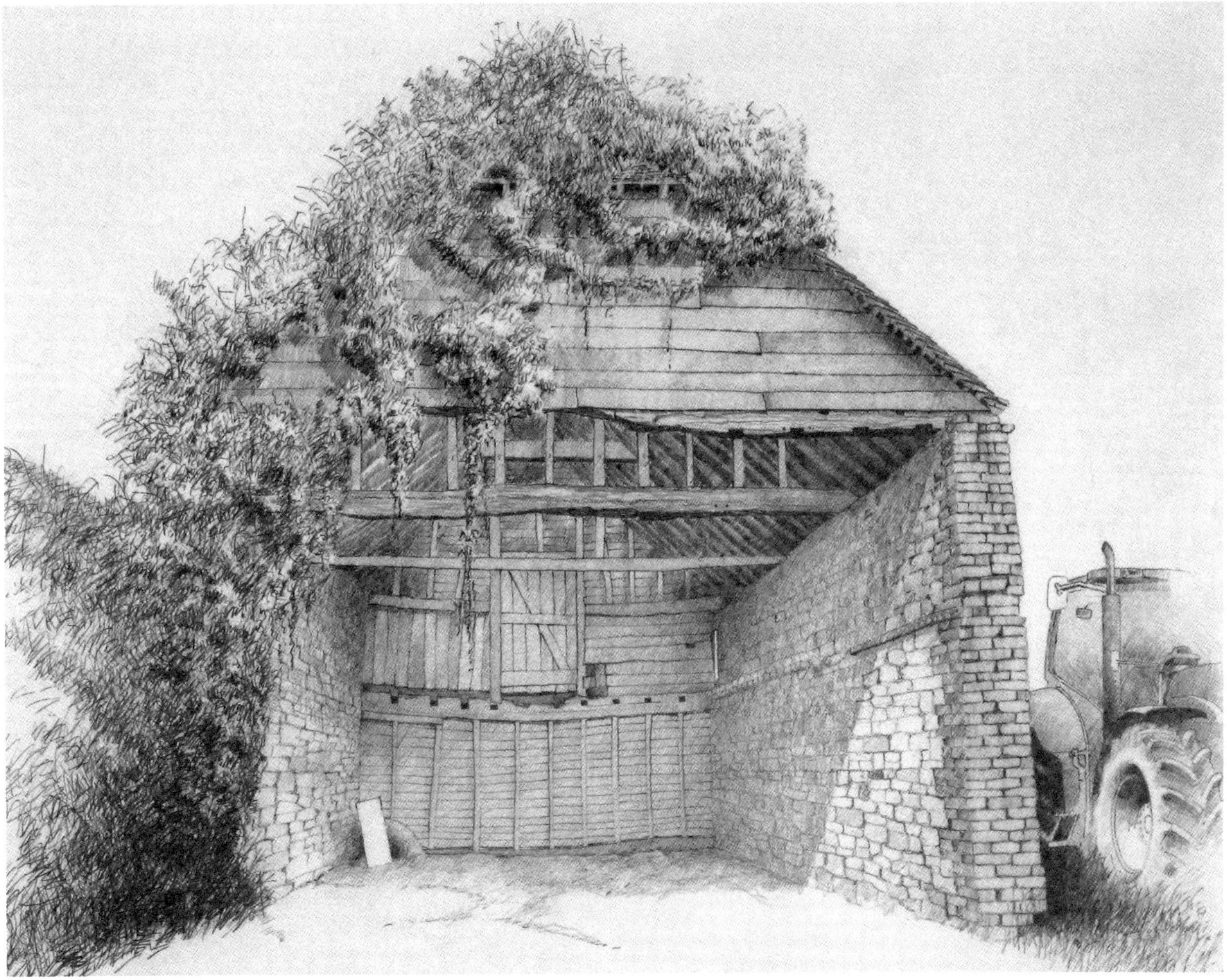

41

Farm buildings near Lurgashall
26.0 × 42.8 cm.

On the pond a skin of scaly duckweed. Broken from time to time by big bubbles wobbling unsteadily to the surface. Decomposition of detritus is all it is but you can't help thinking of a slow old carp or an eel as thick as a child's arm and a wet night and a long journey.

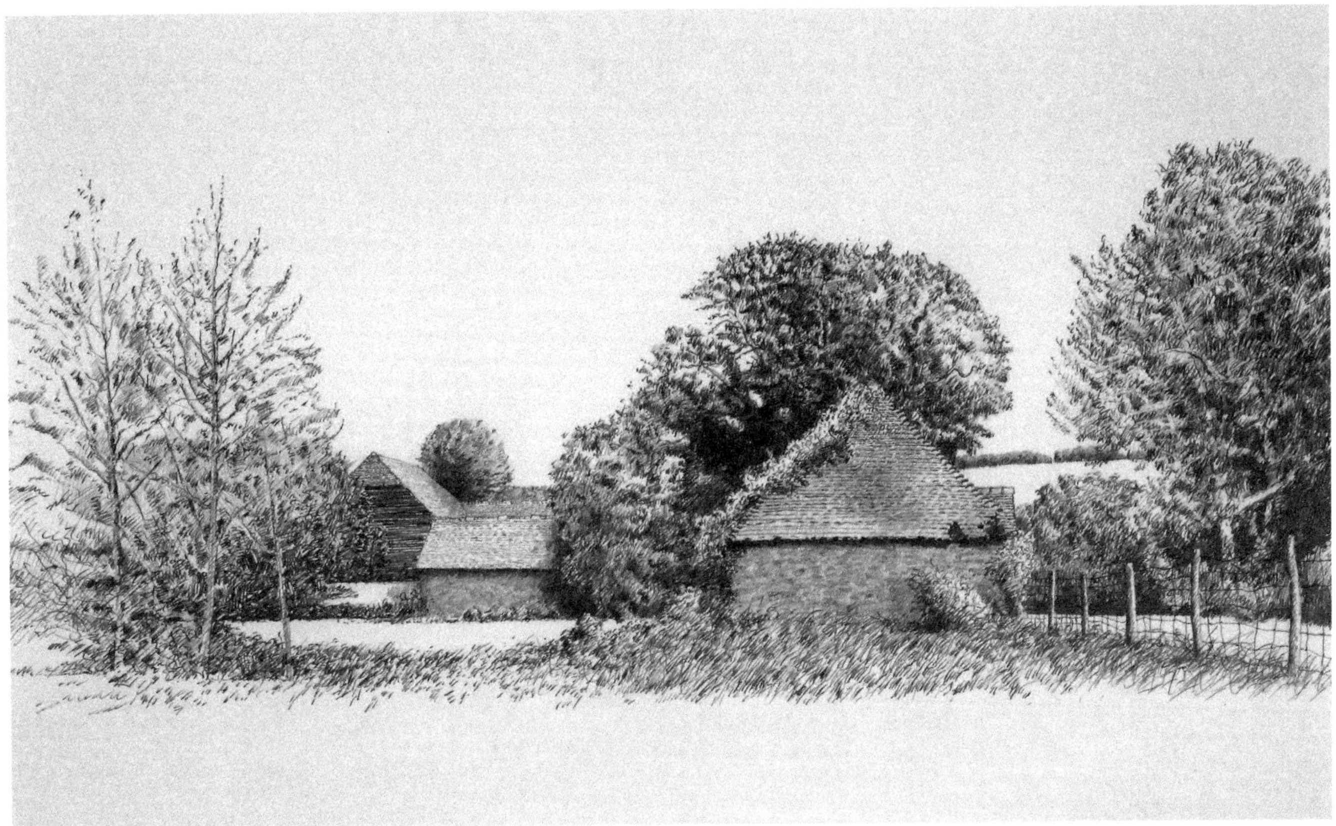

42

Disused granary near Lurgashall (1)
28.5 × 37.7 cm.

Probably I shouldn't be here today. I don't feel well. People are sometimes said to live to fight another day. When you are unwell you fight to live another day. I'm not a fighter but I'm fighting. I'm going to get this drawing done.

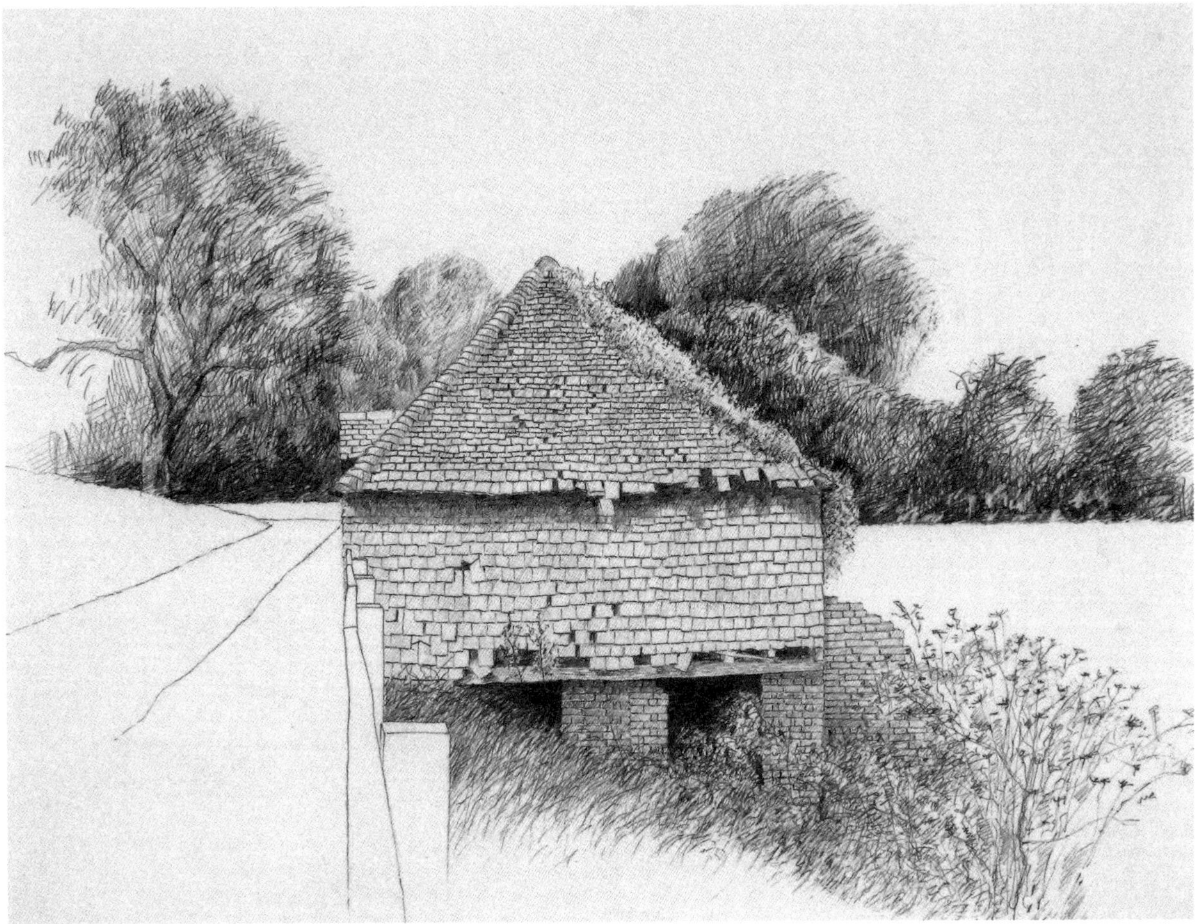

43

Disused granary near Lurgashall (2)
23.6 × 35.5 cm.

However much you think of the past, these drawings are about now. They are about transition and change. Phrases like time warp and nostalgia are not on even the far horizons of my mind.

But I don't know how to define "now." It's a still Sunday afternoon. Lights were switched on early – in houses with wide eaves of dripping thatch they'll have been on all day. Blackbirds shake the droplets on dead-looking branches of buddleia and people are watching *The African Queen* on BBC2. Not me. I'm here. Watching the circles of rain on the surface of the pond. Too wet for pencil and paper but this is still drawing. Drawing is looking and reading and thinking. The marks on the paper merely the proof that it was done. Is that "now"?

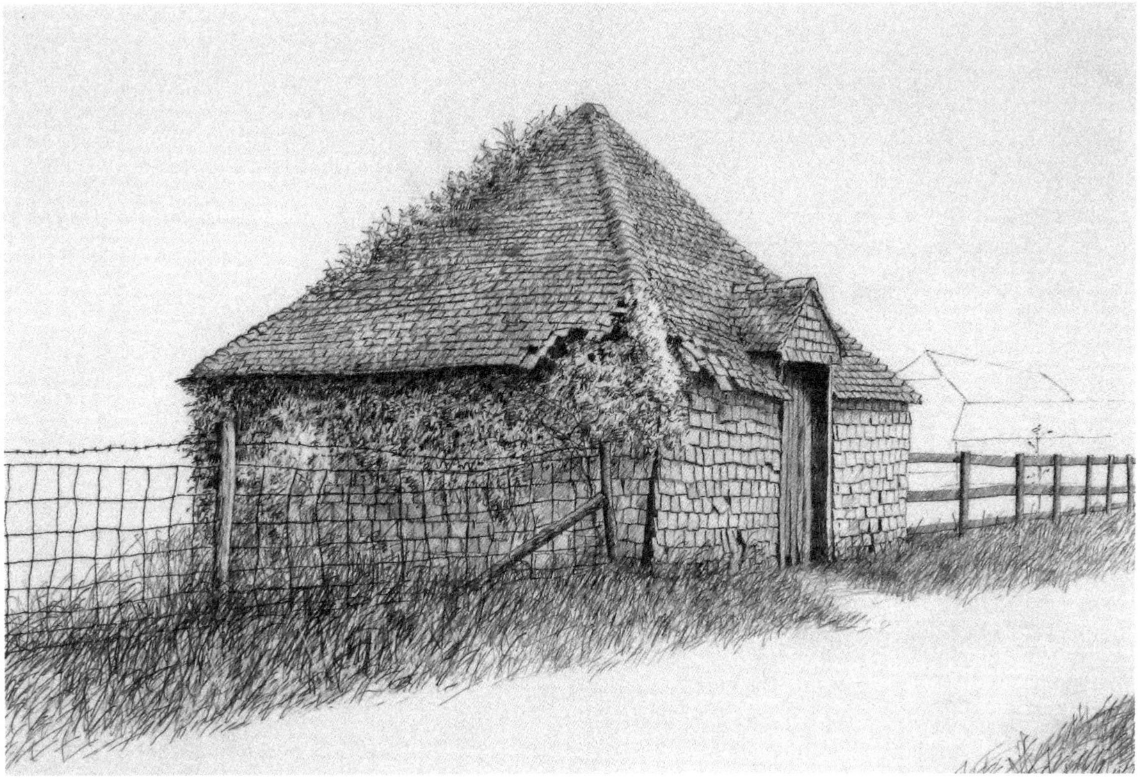

44

Derelict field barn
near Lurgashall
23.5 × 43.5 cm.

It's like a coral reef full of life. A brigantine or a frigate settled for years on the sea bed. The conger and the wrasse don't discriminate between oak ribs and iron fixings. Neither do the chaffinch and the blackcap.

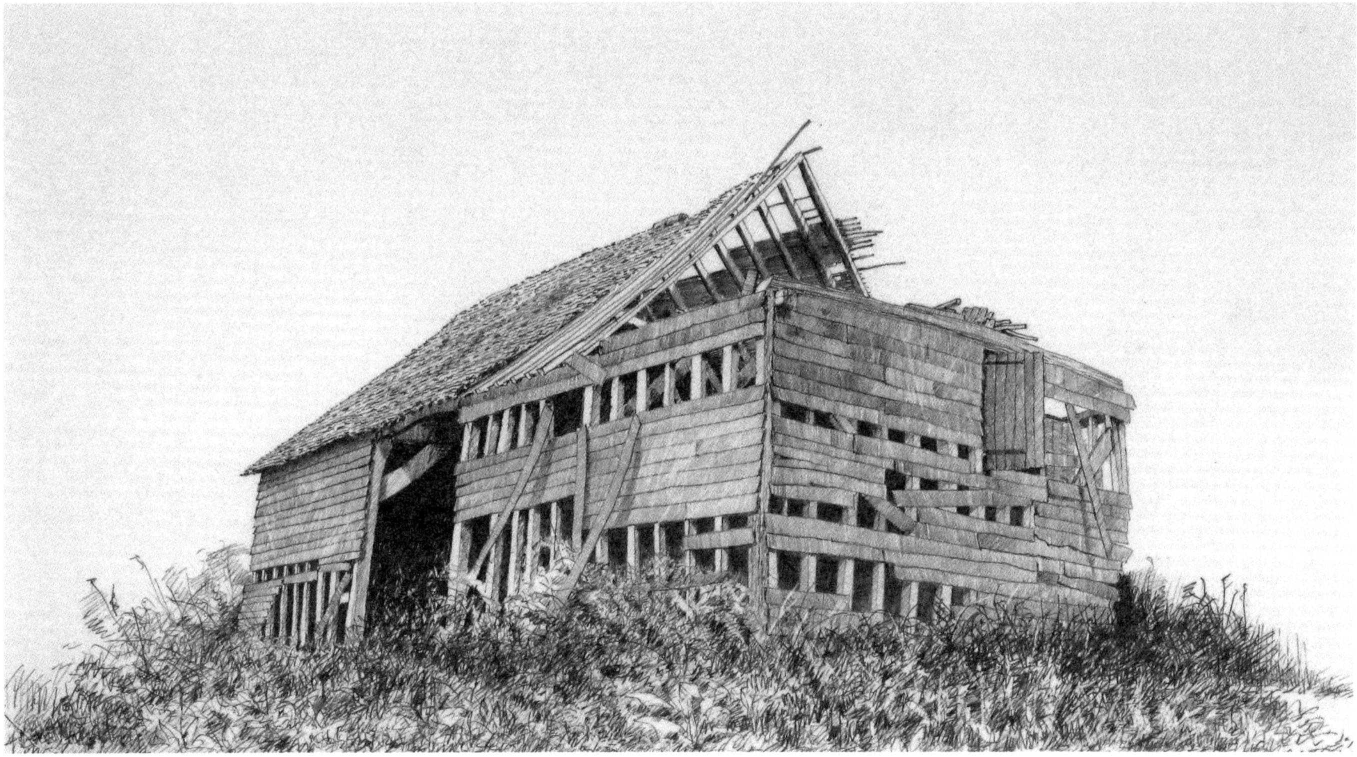

45

Overgrown farm
buildings near
Wisborough Green
26.5 × 41.6 cm.

Two hedge sparrows picking at the bare brown earth, nervous and edgy as mice. Like Kipling's Chuchundra, they are afraid to be in the open. But if you stay still you are unseen or are seen as not to be a threat. There will be a grassy bowl of a nest, all lined with moss and hair among the corrugated iron. Four eggs, blue like the sky in a watercolour.

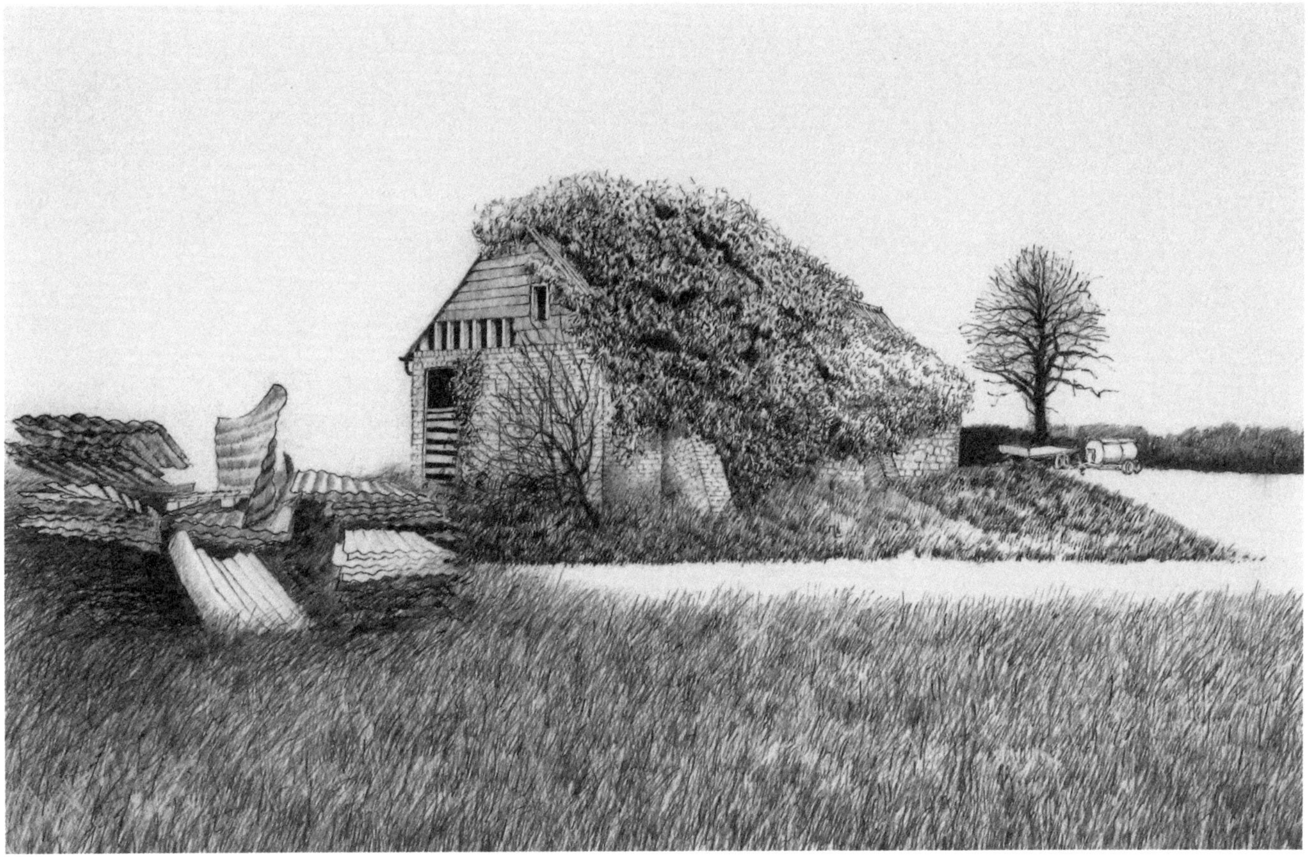

46

Timber framed barn near Wisborough Green
29.0 × 41.8 cm.

How long have I been here?

Have I been here longer than this undulating barn or was it here first? You lose yourself in time. You become time itself. And time doesn't pass – it's always there somewhere. I am Virginia Woolf's radio: "I shall fit a plug into the wall and listen in to the past."

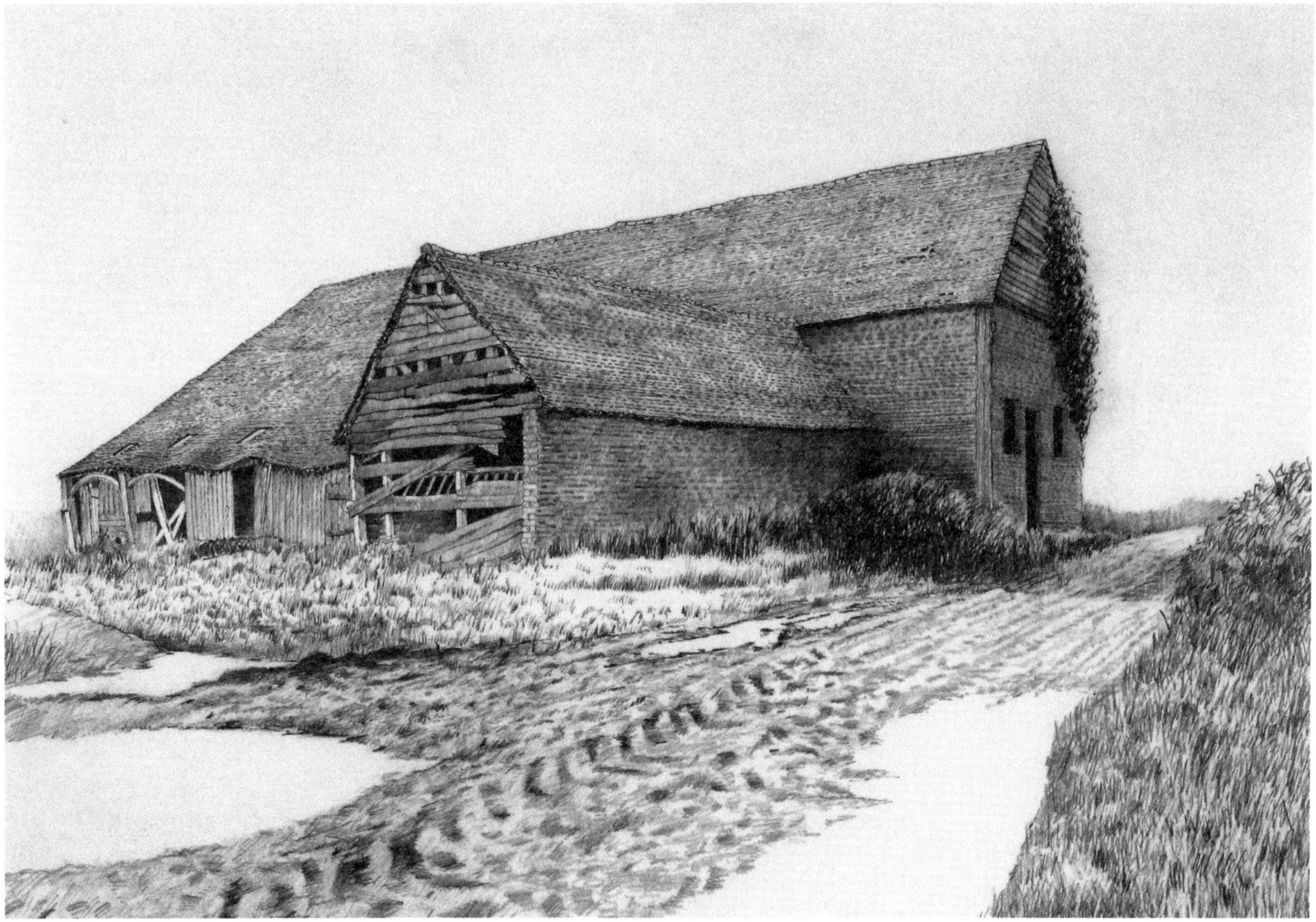

47

Farm buildings near
Wisborough Green
26.5 × 38.8 cm.

Silage in balloon-like plastic. Sometimes black, sometimes pale greenish blue and looking like marshmallows. Balloons and marshmallows tipping the balance of aesthetics. Like in a pretty village where you have a feeling of having eaten too much Turkish delight. But then you drive past a row of bungalows built from cheap bricks. "This is better," you can't help thinking. "This is more like it."

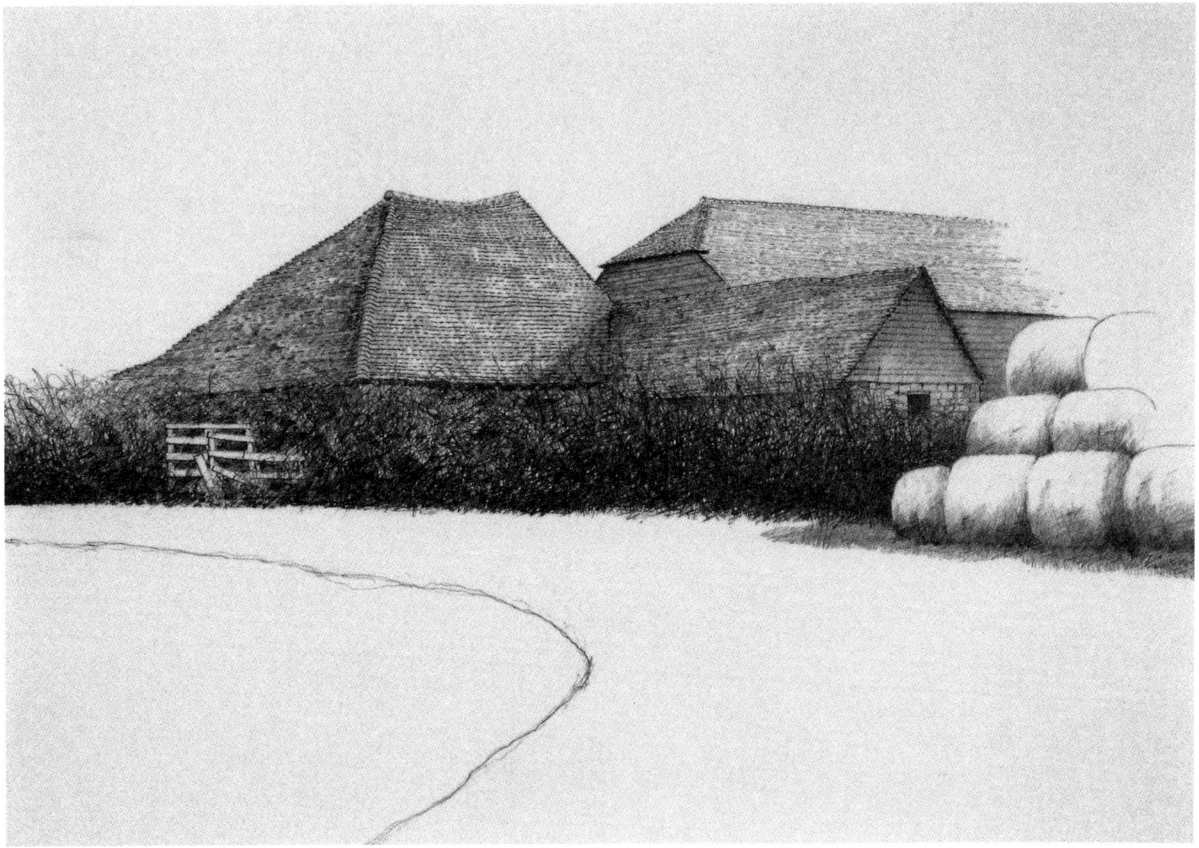

48

Timber framed barn
near Kirdford (1)
27.5 × 42.5 cm.

Slipping tiles are the parenthetical phrases in the long paragraphs of agricultural time.

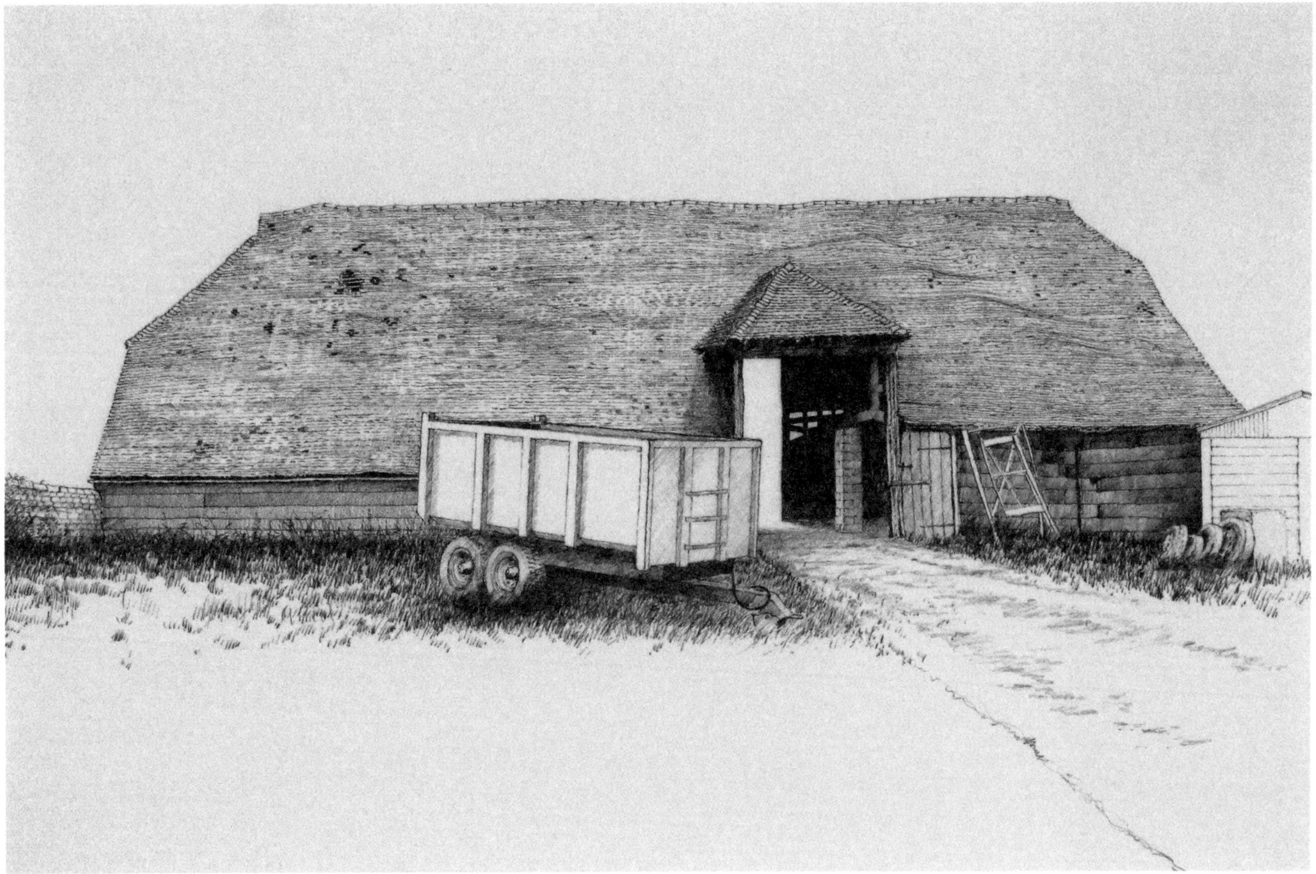

49

Timber framed barn
near Kirdford (2)
27.8 × 36.4 cm.

Sounds trapped in an enclosed yard on a hot, deserted summer Sunday afternoon seem heavy somehow and restless. The unique sound of a bolt sliding somewhere in a door.

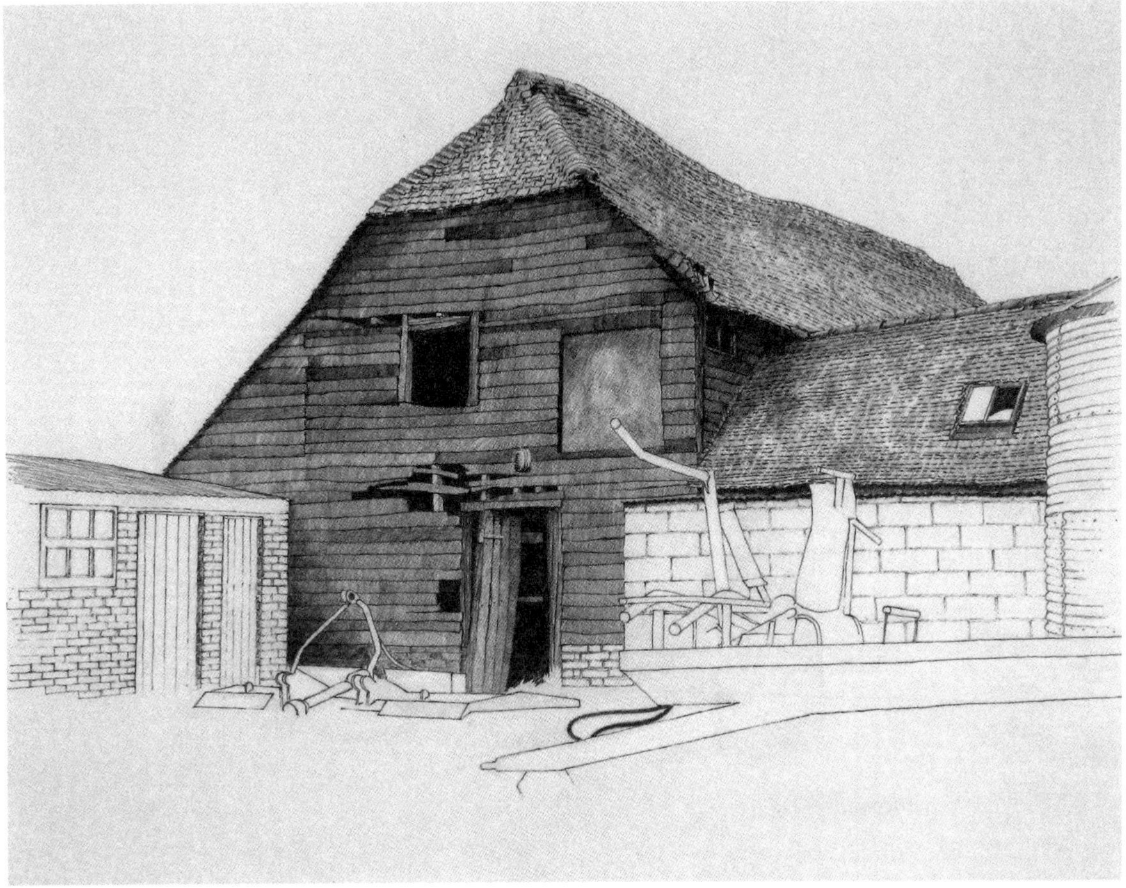

50

Harris's Fun Fair maintenance yard, Ashington
29.0 × 38.7 cm.

There seems to be a fragile allegory of the new world economy and traditional cultures, the one barring the progress or continuation of the other. Yet the typography perhaps suggests something – the weak ephemerality of the computer-generated and the solid trustworthiness of the hand-crafted. It's a long shot but you never know.

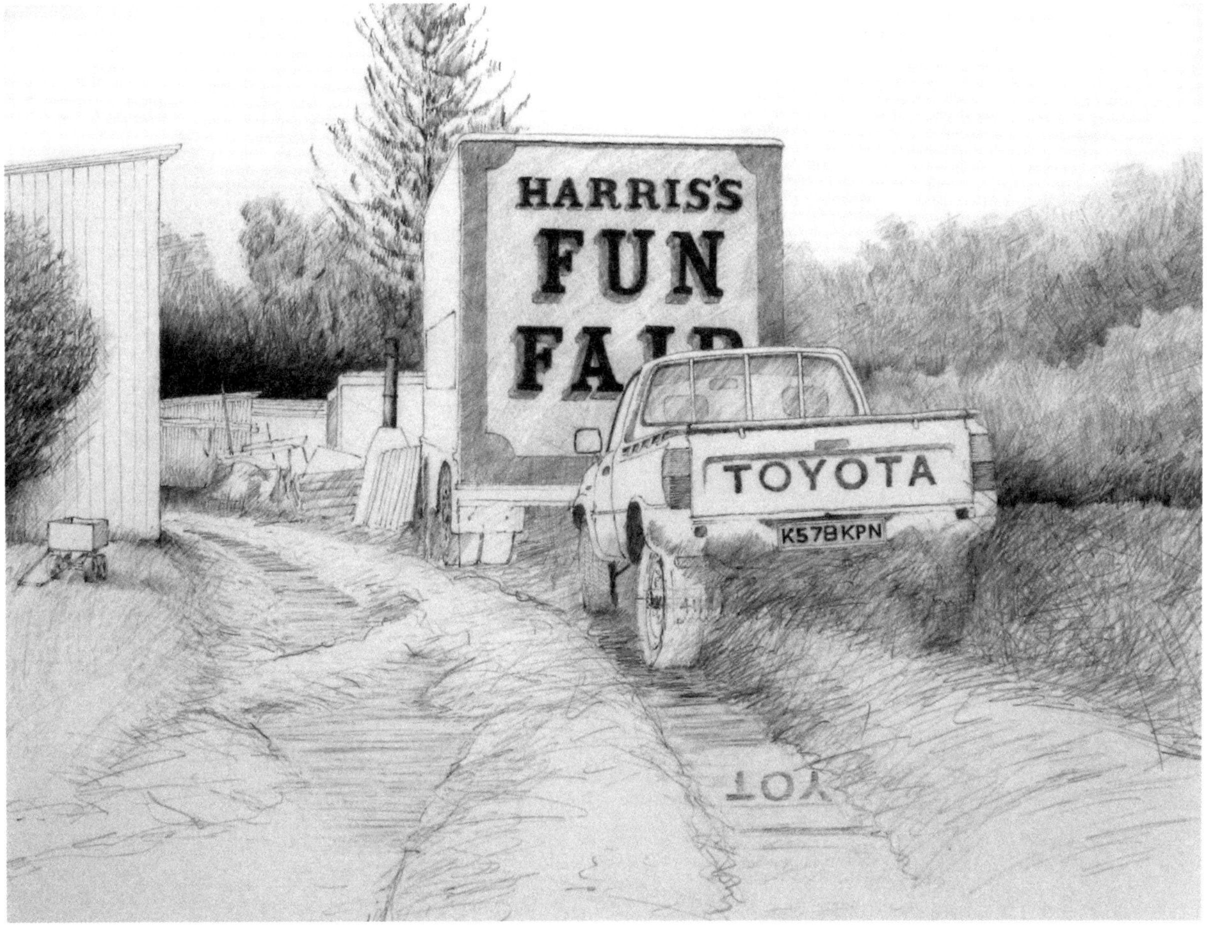
HARRIS'S
FUN
TOYOTA
K578KPN

51

Parkhurst Farmhouse,
Upperton
24.0 × 36.0 cm.
(Private collection)

A late hogweed, its stem coarse and blistering, grows through a beautiful tangle of fence posts and wire. But how surprisingly delicate the tiny white flowers. Their outer petals are longer than the others as if to make the most of the light of the darkening days without crowding its neighbour. You think of the paper doilies in the front room of an aunt who always wore lipstick and who died a long time ago.

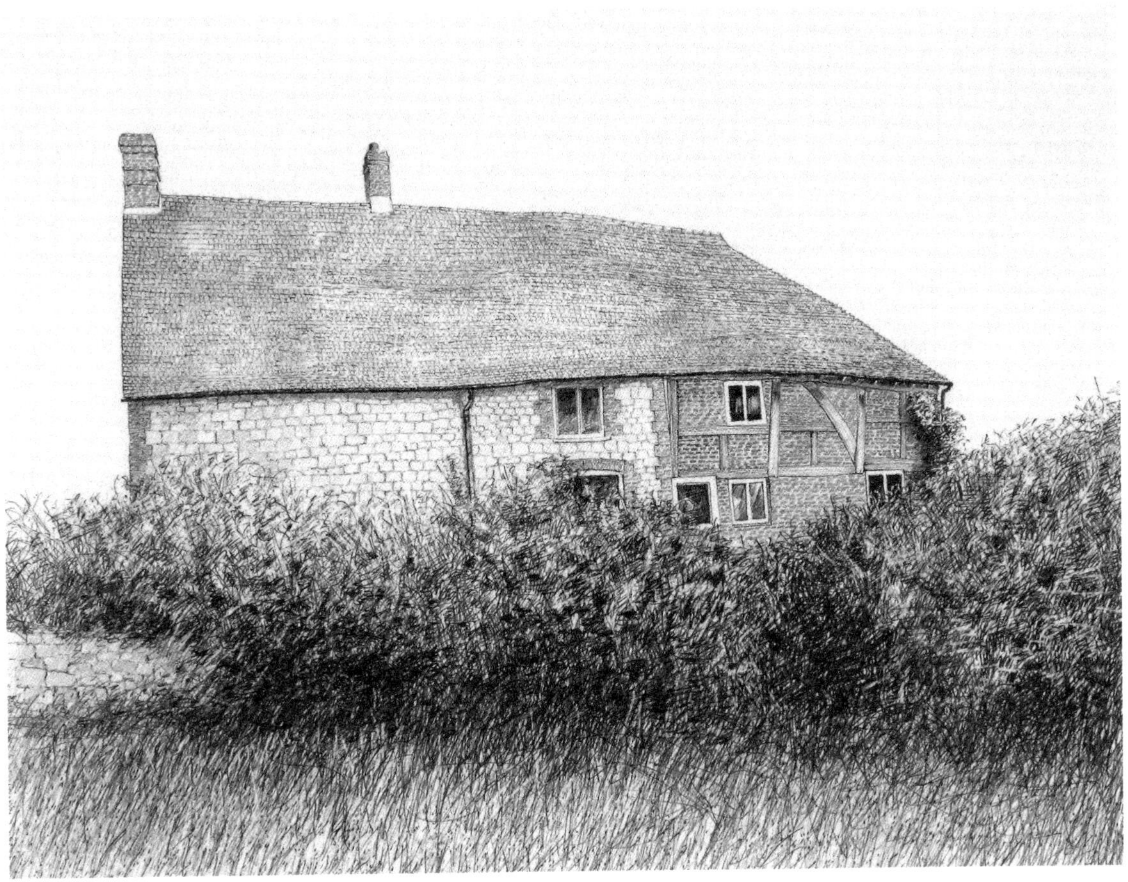

52

Redundant granary near Kirdford
26.5 × 44.2 cm.

I like the way you can read history through buildings and architecture, but will this branch of history reading be applicable to the years following the second world war? Will the buildings we are making today last to tell the histories of their time? Will this aspect of history-reading show a void, a hole of nothingness? Does this matter?

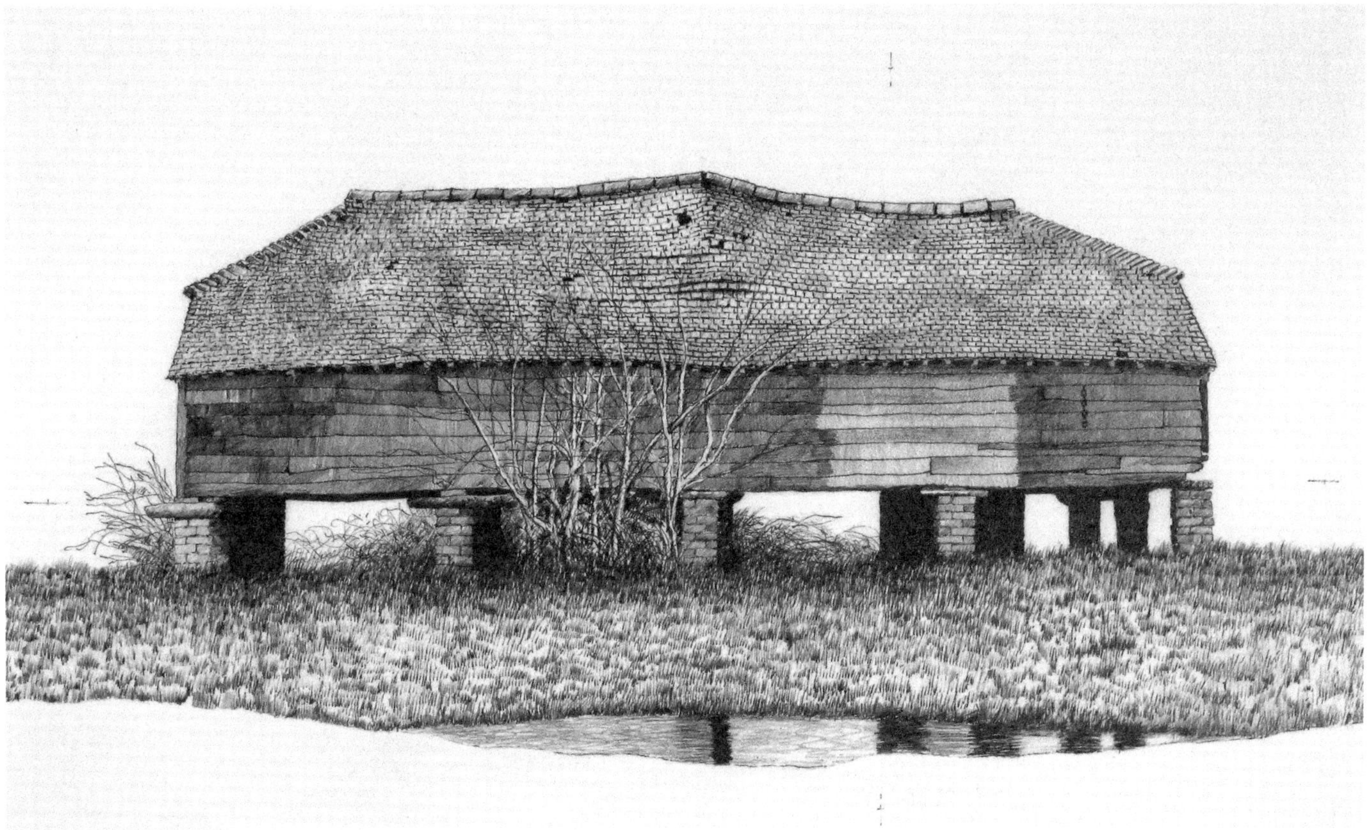

53

Timber framed barn converted to a Dutch barn near Kirdford
29.8 × 46.0 cm.

These are industrial buildings, for farming has always been an industry. An industry as a symbiosis between the farmer, political governments, the government of nature and the laws of God. But nature and God seem now to be given less of an opinion than they were once allowed.

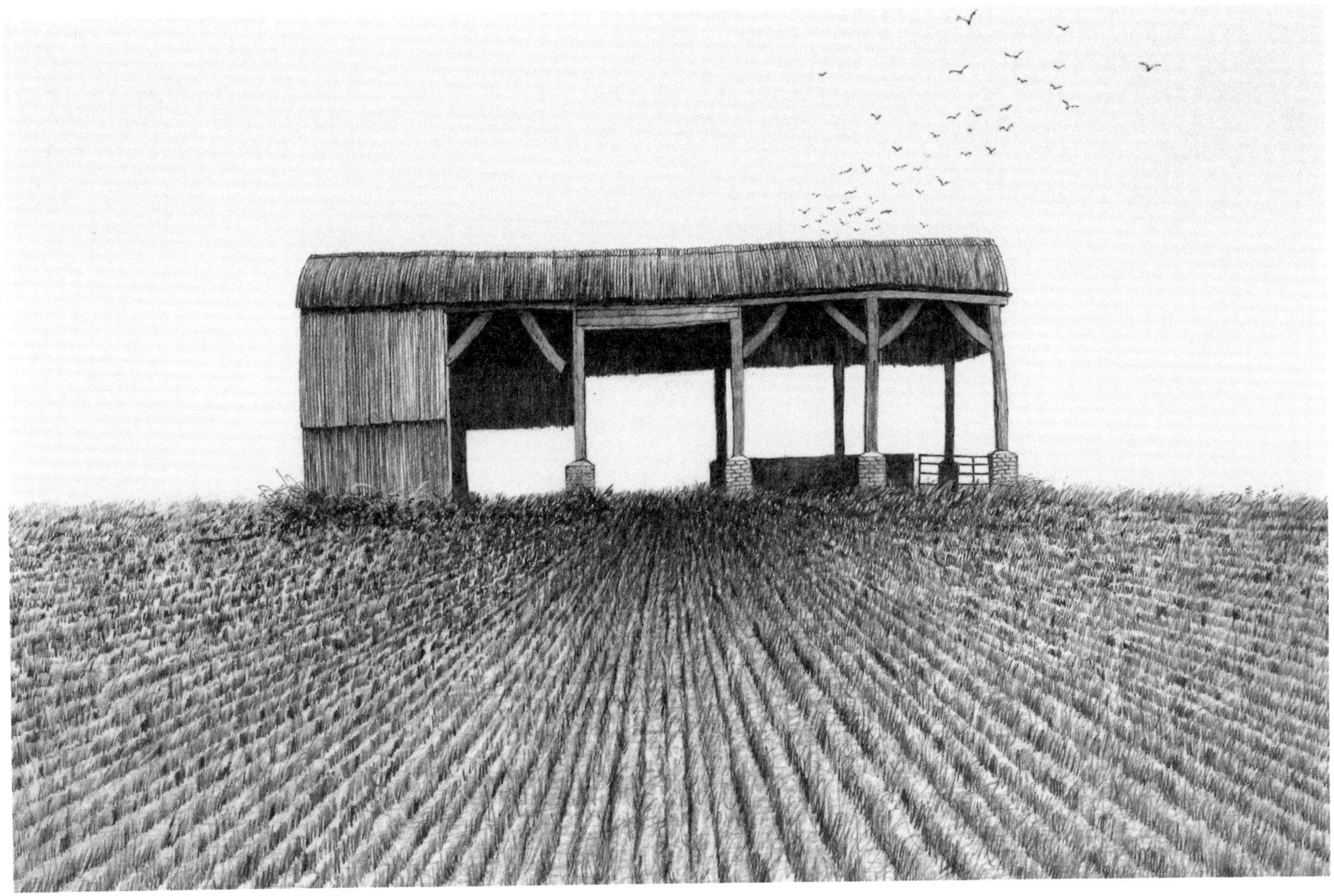

54

Barns at Lickfold
32.2 × 42.1 cm.

Sometimes, for no sensible reason, you just want to be somewhere else. Driving a canary-yellow Chevrolet with red seats down some wide boulevard with palm trees and the sun so bright that the neon signs cannot compete. An off-duty cheer-leader glides past on roller skates and Mr Hockney greets Mr Blake.

Something, you don't know what, returns you to reality. It's good to be back.

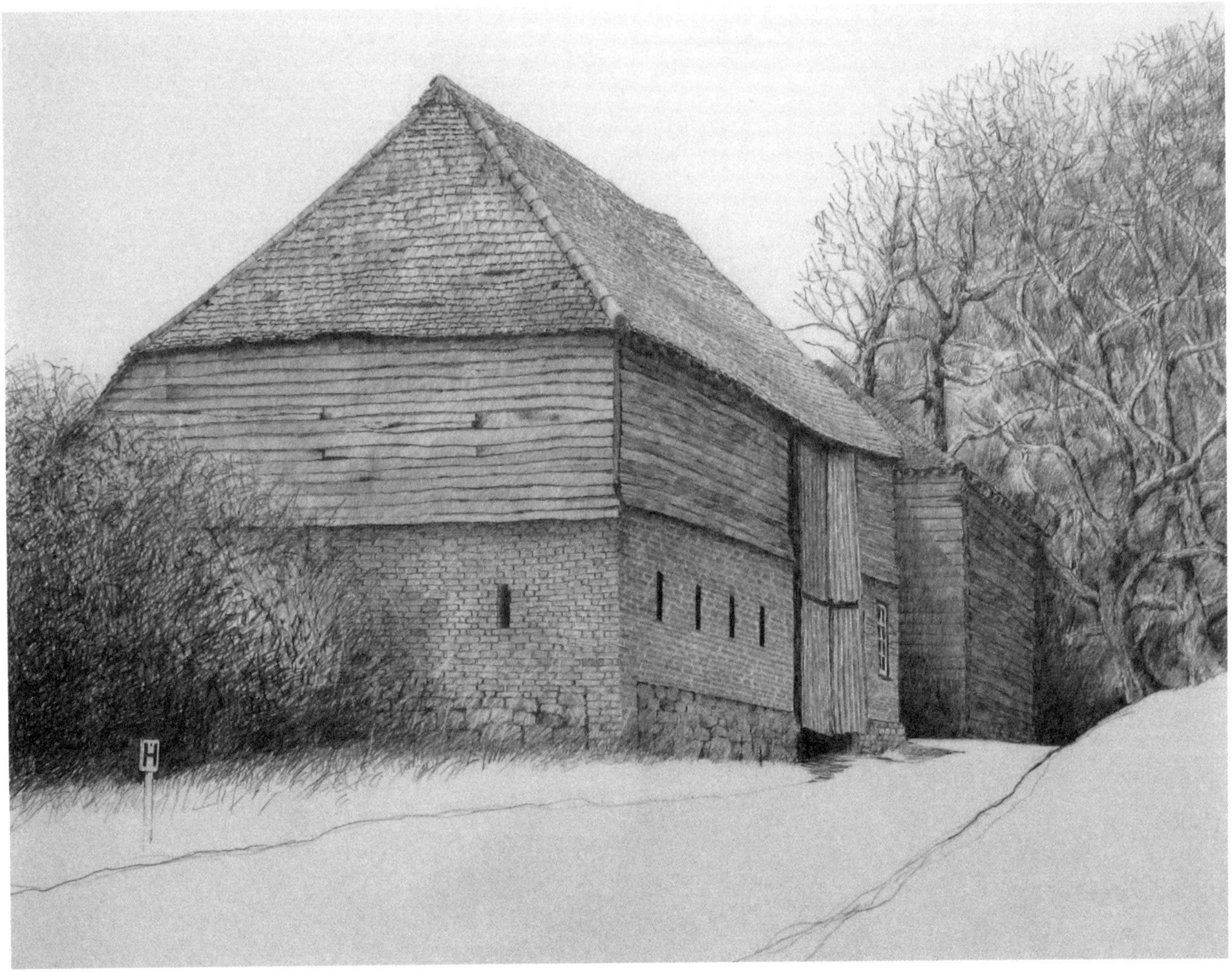
H

55

Brick building at Lickfold
26.0 × 41.0 cm.

I think sometimes that in another life I should have been a part time parson: Trollope's lepidopterist on the edge of Lake Como, Francis Kilvert, Gilbert White, W. Keble Martin. A life spent recording the everyday, the ordinary, the apparently insignificant. To be sort of ecclesiastical Sir Alister Hardy with push-bike and a net at the side of a canal and taste strawberries still warm from the sun as the curate does his rounds and spends too much time with the bailiff's daughter.

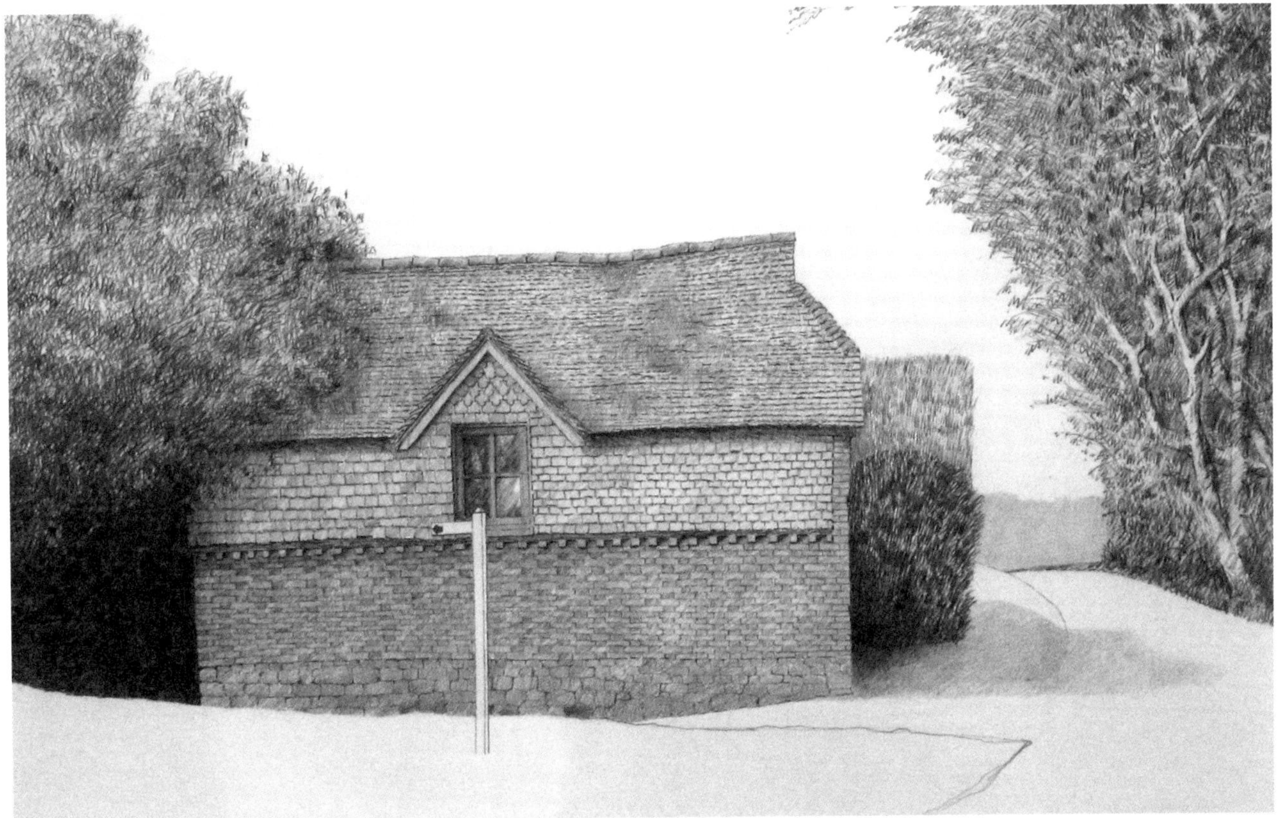

56

Timber framed barn under repair near Balls Cross (1)
28.5 × 44.5 cm.

These drawings seem to suggest architectural and topographical truths. But it isn't always so. I may, without question, add features which are not there in reality (but which may have been yesterday or could be tomorrow). Equally I will omit things. Neither am I much concerned with truthfulness to light and shade. The drawings take a long time and the sun moves across the sky more quickly than I can move across the paper. It's not unusual for shadows to fall from left to right on one part of the drawing and from right to left on another part. I am not looking to capture a moment in time.

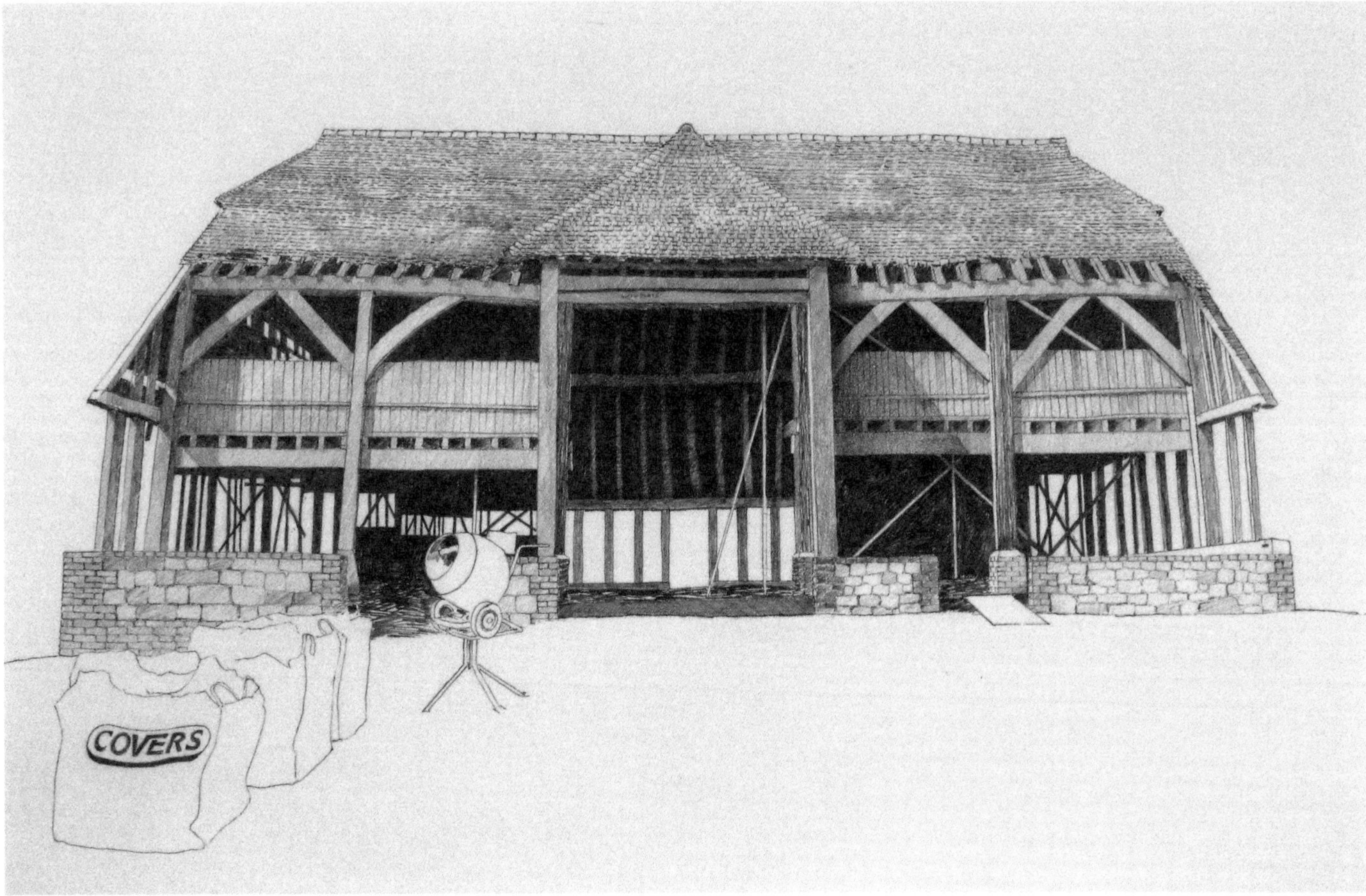
COVERS

57

Timber framed barn
under repair near
Balls Cross (2)
25.7 × 43.2 cm.

The drawings are not planned. There is no pre-ordained scheme. They happen, that's all. I have no idea how they will develop and this seems to be a metaphor for the uncertainties of the world in which their subjects anachronistically remain. Yet (and this is not a contradiction) there is for me a sort of unforeseen inevitability within the lack of planning. I didn't know, for instance, that the helicopter would fly across my line of sight, nor that in other drawings I would include a tangle of brambles or a barrier of wire netting. But when I found that these were going in to the drawings I realised that it was inevitable.

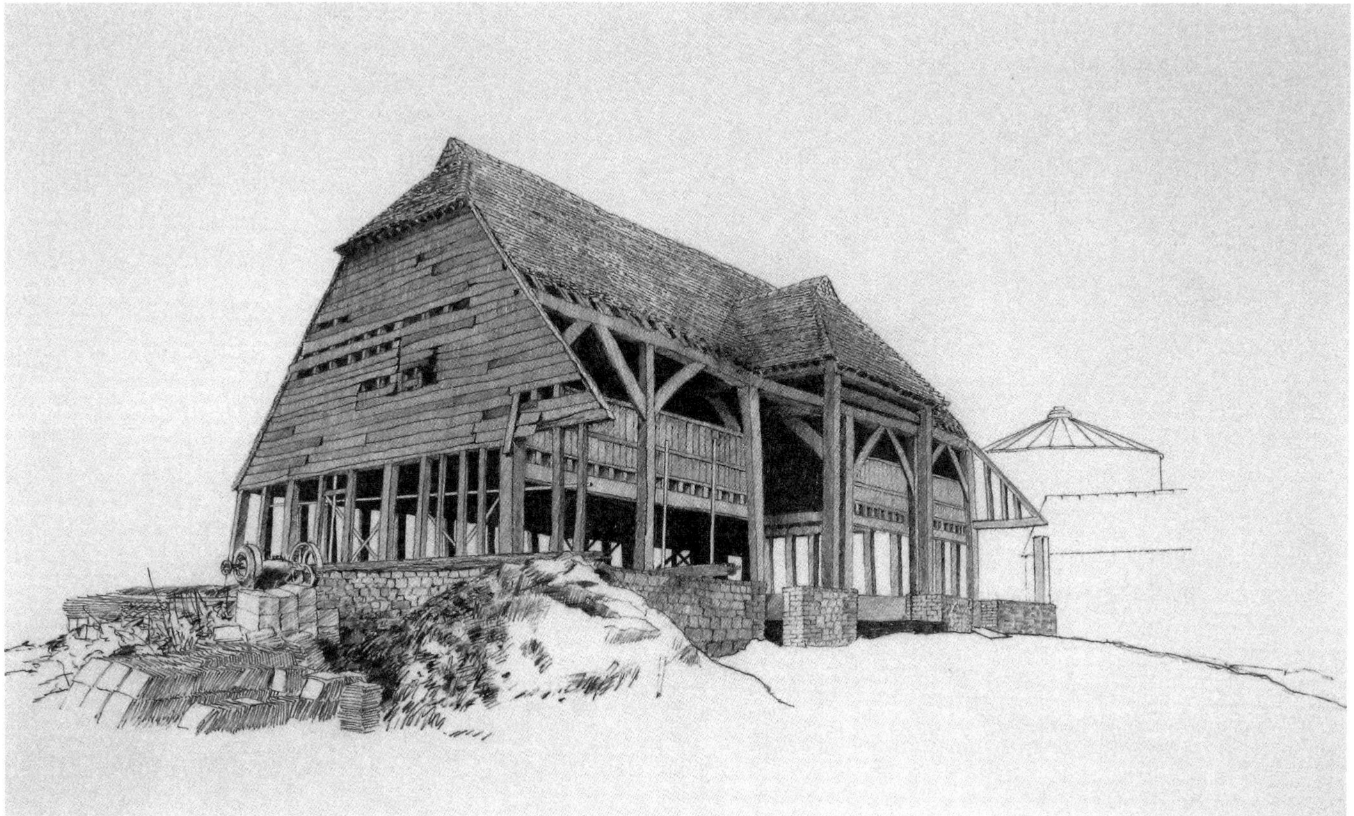

58

Timber framed barn under repair near Balls Cross (3)
27.5 × 44.7 cm.

My drawings of sheds, hovels and barns may appear to be accurate renditions of big things miniaturised but that's the result of my careful line. Things are not always what they seem and, like the door-to-door salesman, they do sometimes tell a convincing but different story.

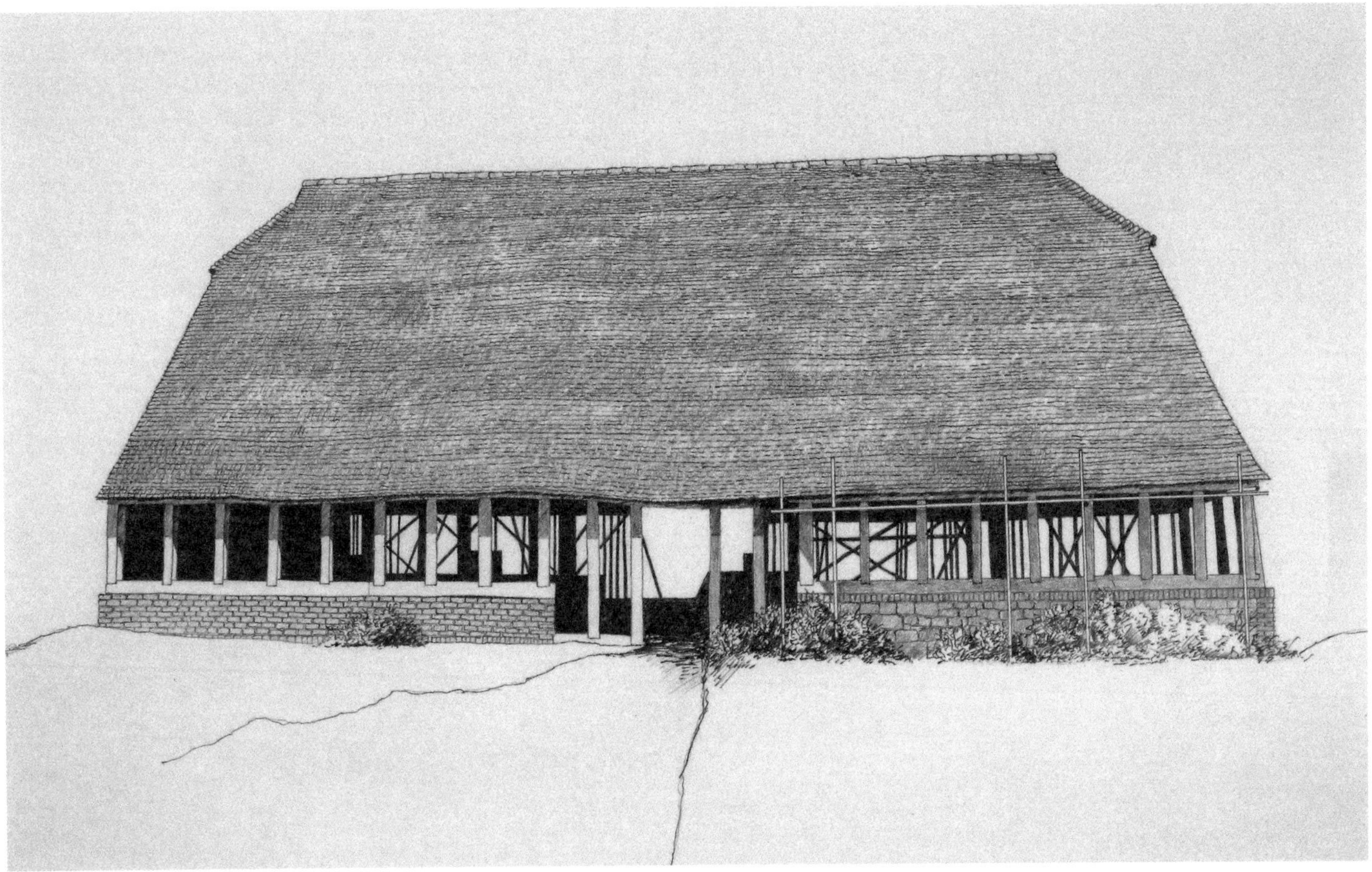

59

Estate yard, Petworth
24.5 × 44.0 cm.

If a maintenance yard of a great estate in a small town can be described as urban, then this is about as urban as I get. The real tennis court building rising behind like a ship stranded in dry dock. The players in their whites, the painters and decorators in theirs. Piles of bricks, timber under cover and broken Rayburns. A van delivering plumbing fittings – gate valves and pipework. "Sign here. No, that's ours. You keep the pink one."

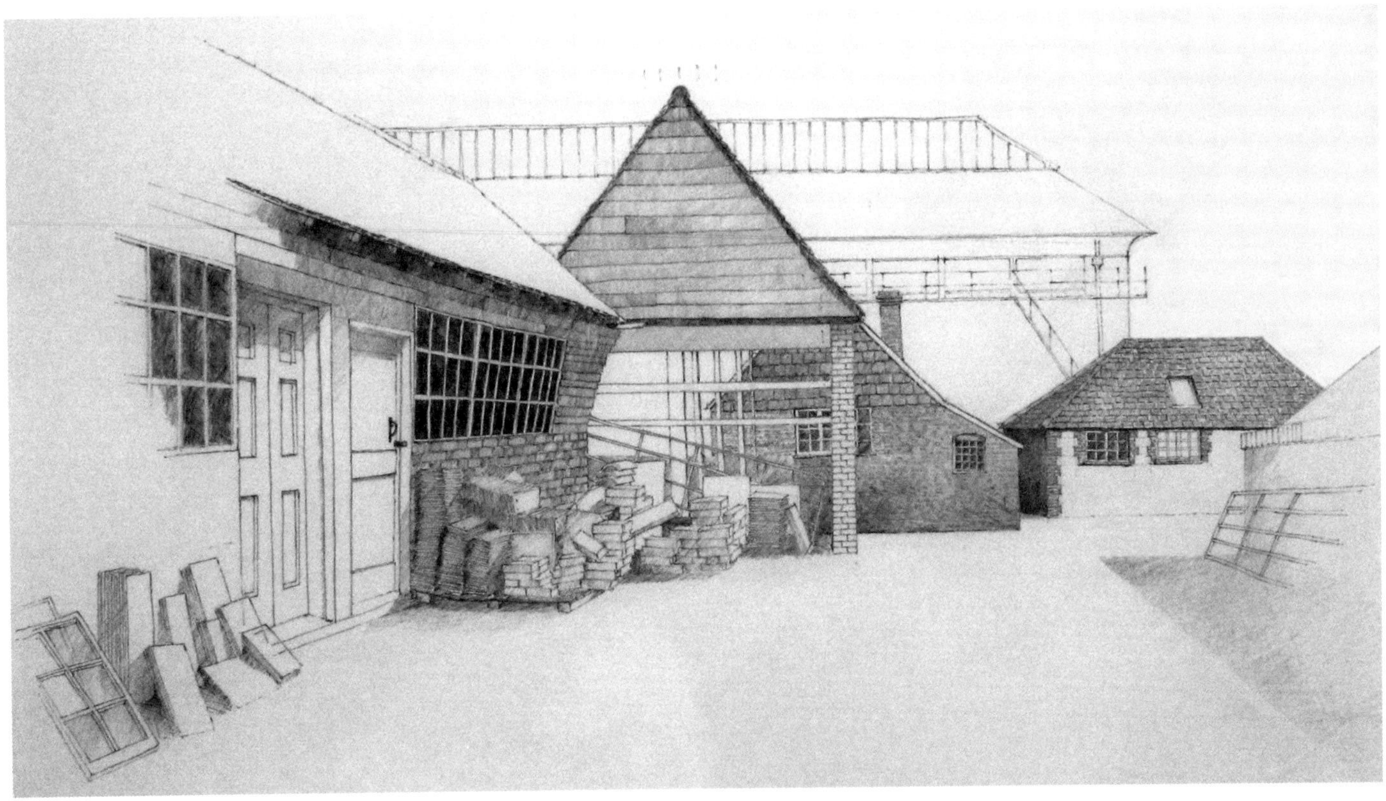

60

Stone barn near Lurgashall
23.6 × 39.2 cm.

A white plastic bucket, full of water with a thin film of ice. It holds back the gate. On its side someone has written, quite neatly in black: "Air Ambulance Fund." You can hear it being shaken with its coins at a charity run.

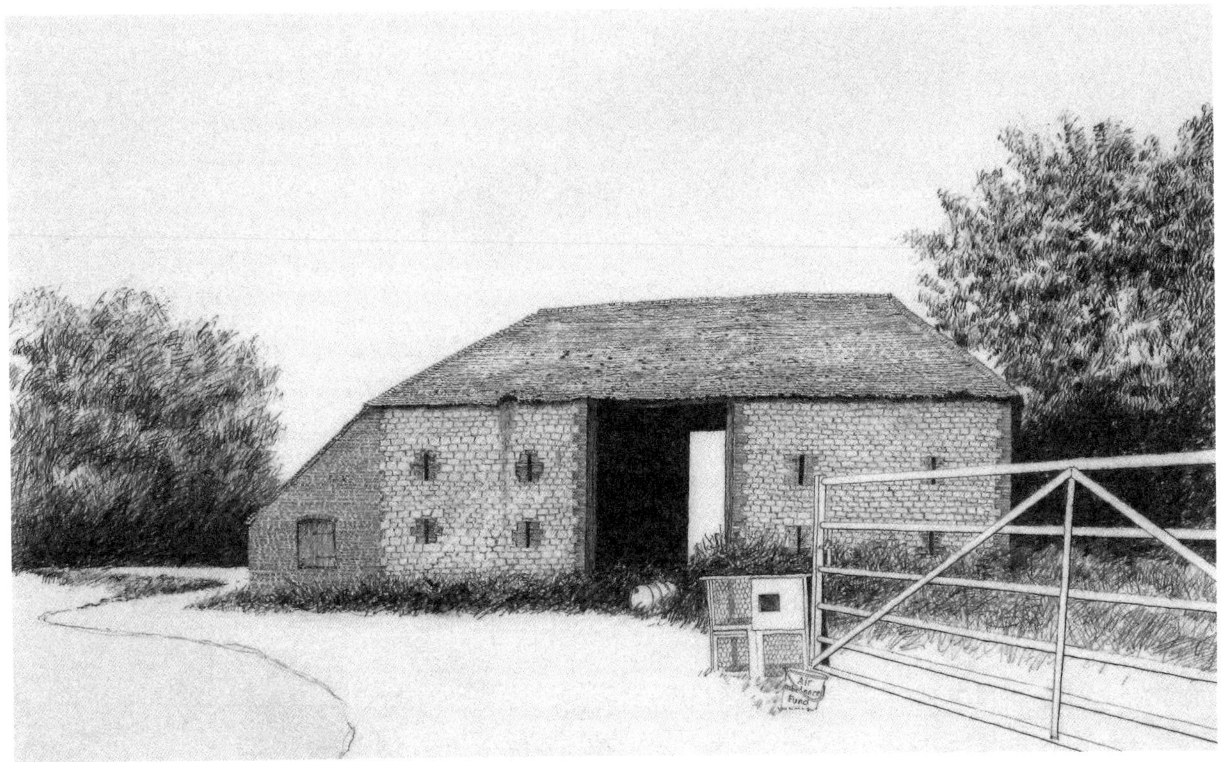
Air
Fund

61

Stone barn and stock yard near Lurgashall
27.0 × 36.5 cm.

The gamekeeper said I should come here and the gamekeeper was right. But I'd forgotten I'd been here before. It's like being woken from a dream – or being thrown back into one. Not asking if that's where you want to be. Is this what Charles Ryder felt?

"... You never saw such a thing."

"Yes, Hooper, I did. I've been here before." There were new lambs and the air was heavy with the scent of bluebells.

But there's work to be done.

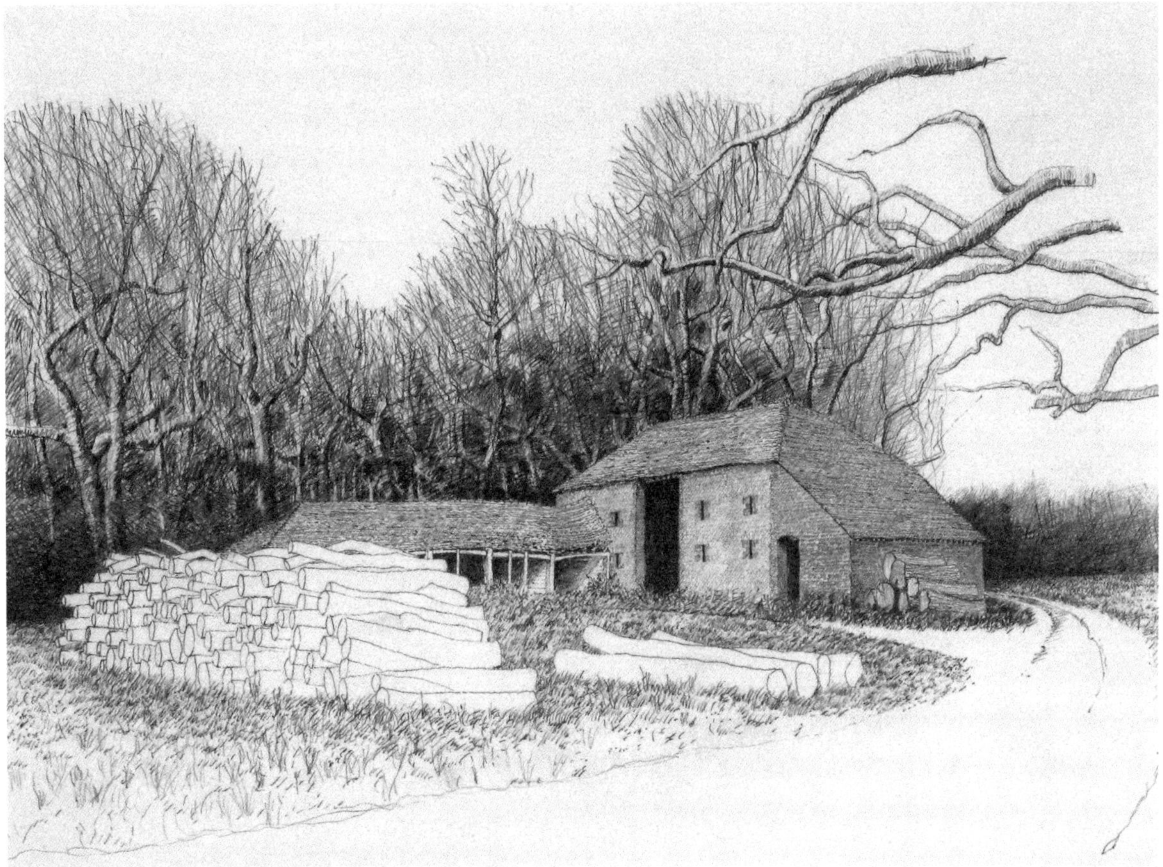

62

Rotherbridge Farm,
Petworth
31.0 × 48.0 cm.

Walking through the morning mist to the drawing (I often think of the site of the drawing as one and the same thing as the marks on my paper).

Already, among the pointed green leaves of dog's mercury, the snowdrop petals are turning brown, and I'm thinking how would it be if the drawing didn't see me coming? If I were to surprise it, would it look different from the way it looked yesterday?

At art college some of us were advised to read essays by Lacan, Derrida (what my wise and pragmatic maternal grandmother might have called "a lot of Tommy-Rot") and some of us made the foolish mistake of doing so. Is it the residue of translated French that causes me to think this way? I don't know but I do know that it is like creeping up on God and trying to catch him out. You can't do it.

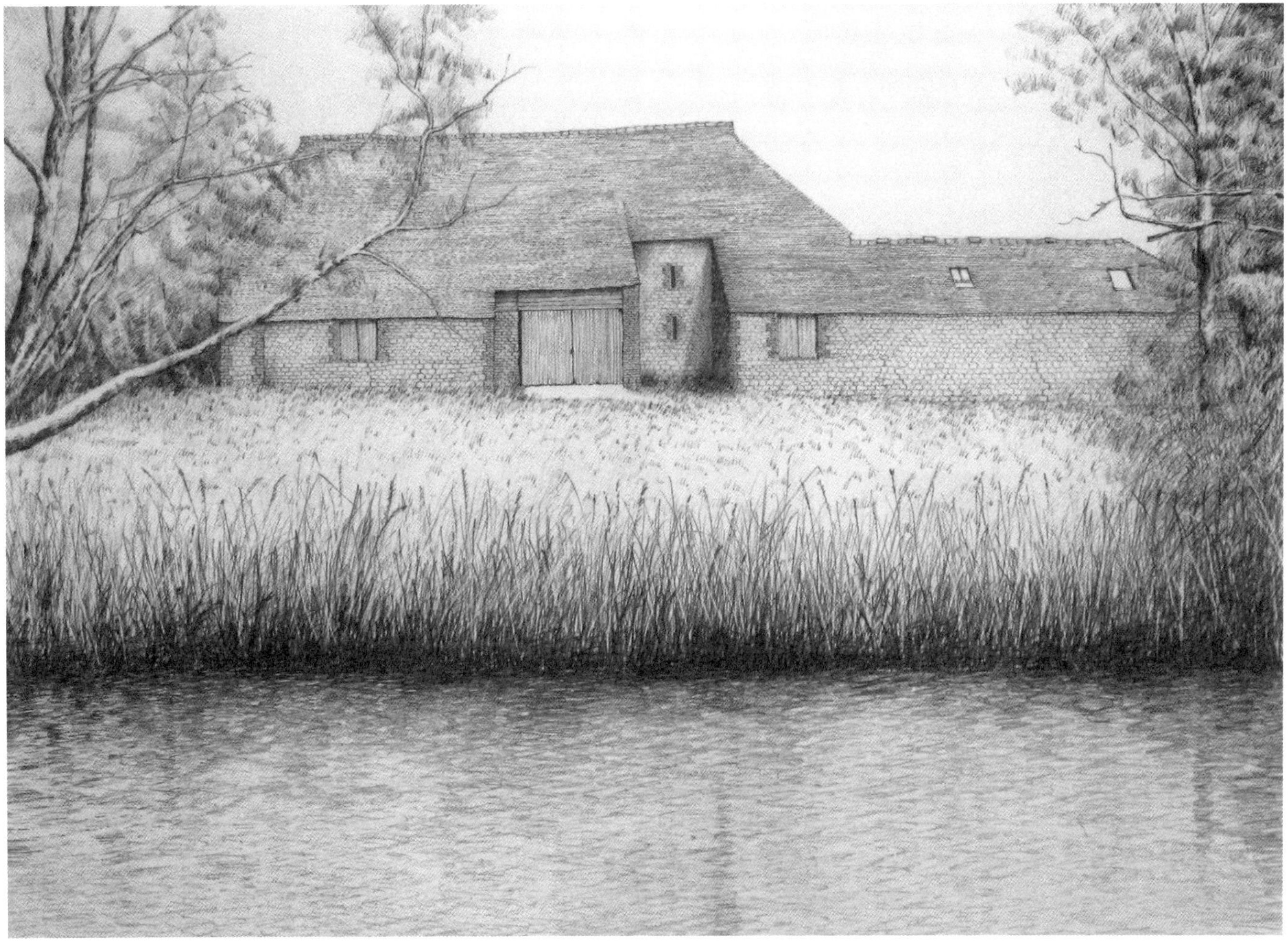

63

Stone barn and stock yard near Tillington (1)
23.8 × 41.8 cm.

These are the new farmers. Plump, shiny men who look as if they've just stepped out of the shower. They drive black Range-Rovers, air-conditioned and are usually on the telephone.

"Hello Gordon," from the open electric window. He's not talking to me – probably he hasn't seen me. It's better that way. The dust settles.

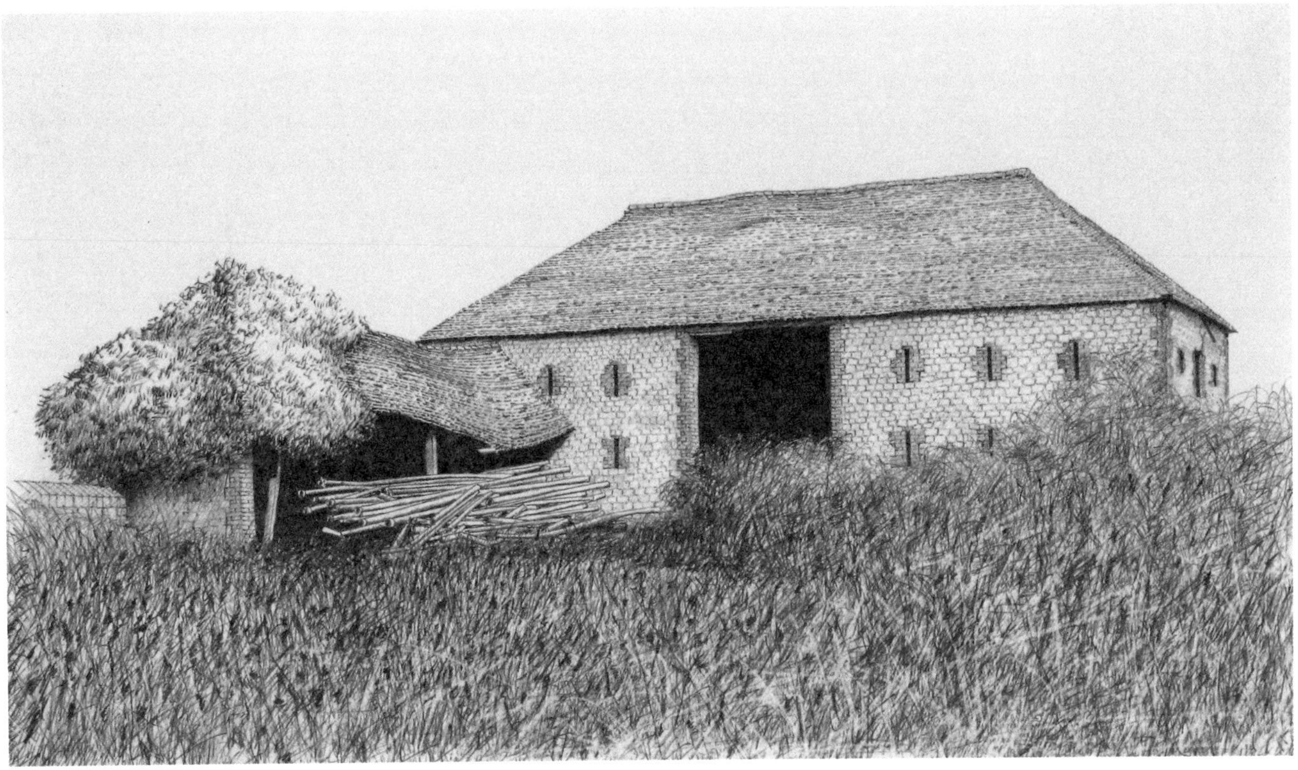

64

Stone shed near Tillington
29.8 × 47.6 cm.

Antoine de Saint-Exupéry wrote that perfection is gained not when there is nothing more to add, but when there is nothing more to take away. I think of this as I make the drawing. He's right, of course he is. Hundred per cent. But, like thinking about landscape which is defined by what is not happening, it does make life difficult.

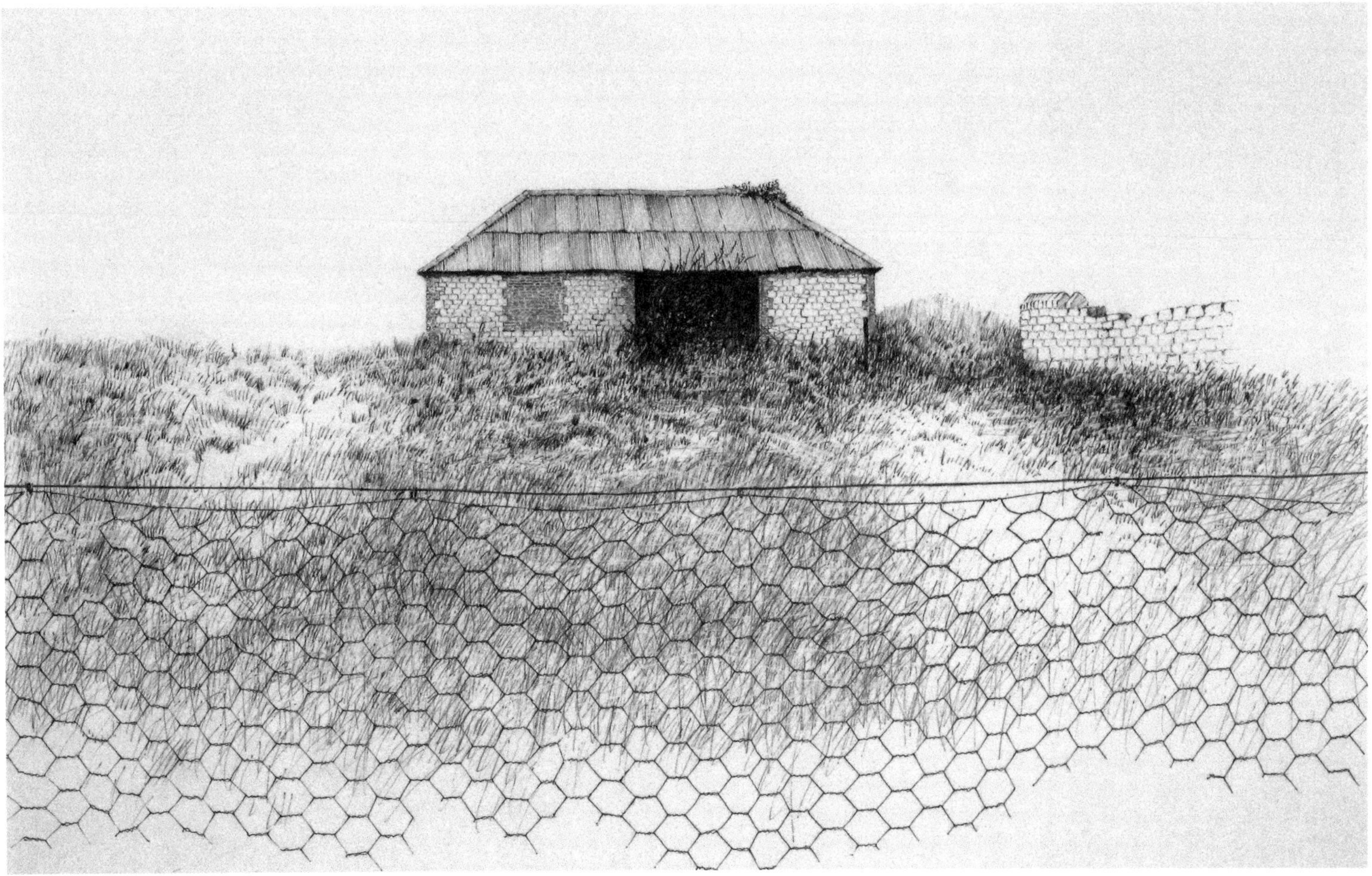

65

Stone barn and stock yard near Tillington (2)
24.8 × 43.2 cm.

I live increasingly with a respect for the 1950s. Your uncle would say "I think I'll take the car out on Sunday if it's fine." Now, half a century later we take the car out as naturally as slipping on our shoes.

But I try not to drive to a drawing. I need to slowly assimilate myself with the place. It's not to avoid catching it unawares like a paparazzo but it's to gently introduce yourself. To begin to know its nuances, to discover what I expect from it and to discover what it might expect from me. It's a relationship. Animate/inanimate but a relationship nonetheless.

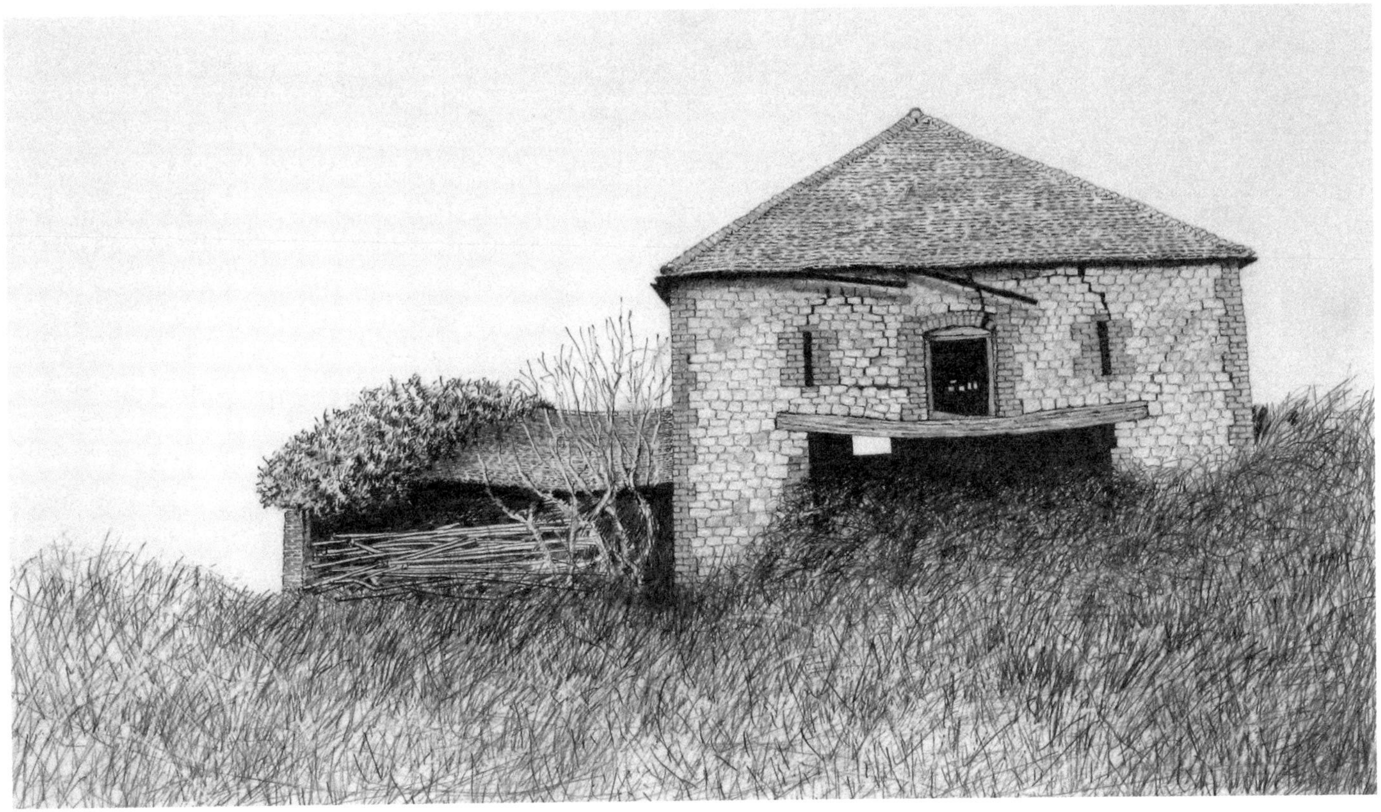

66

Stone barn and stock yard near Tillington (3)
24.0 × 40.0 cm.

This drawing business is like driving an unreliable car along an unknown road at night. You are in constant fear of breakdown. And you wonder, if you switch off, will it start again. There is the fear also of taking a wrong turning and not finding your way back to the right road. And never being completely assured that it is the right road anyway.

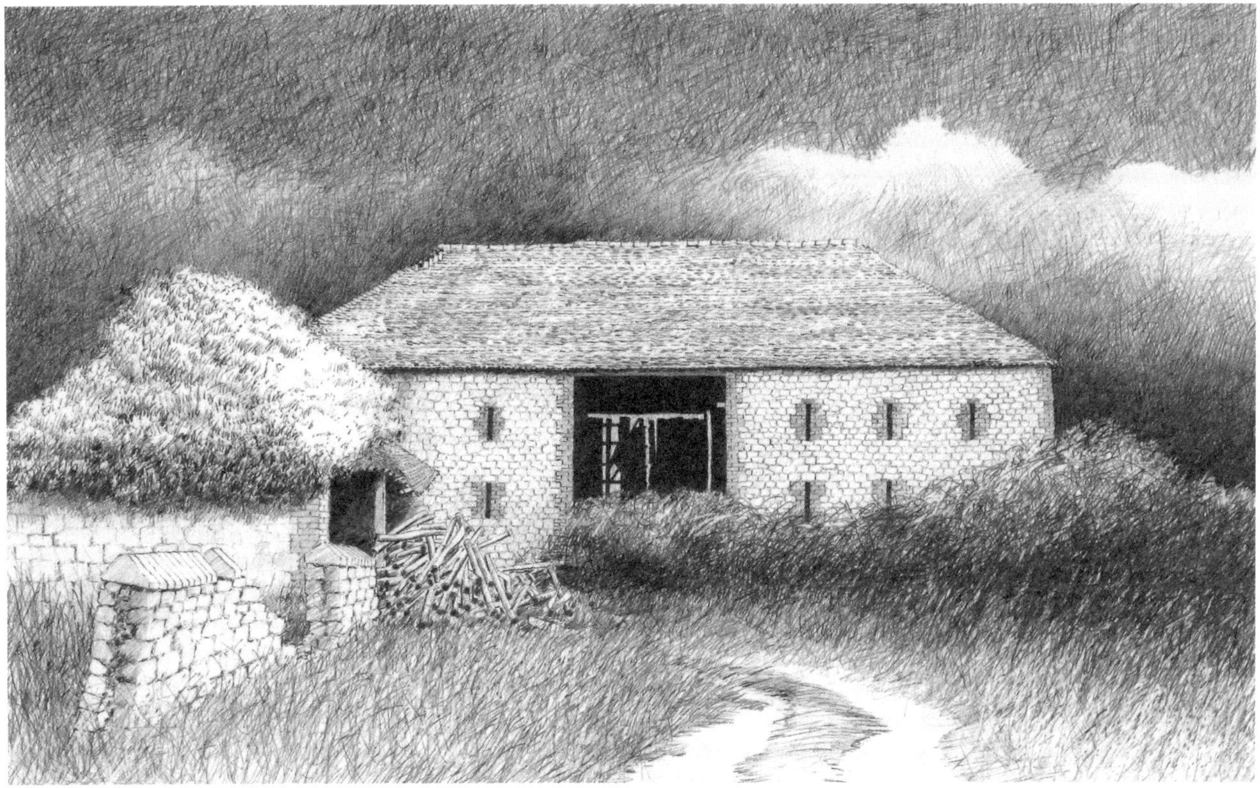

POSTSCRIPT

Barn conversion, Sidlesham
Both 23.0 × 38.5 cm.

These two drawings may, in a few particulars, be somewhat conjectural. The reason being that both were made from photographs, one out of necessity, the other from choice. Both are of the same building (more or less) which is, or was, a late sixteenth-century barn, aisled on all four sides. It is not easy to date a building which conforms to a long established and only gradually changing tradition of vernacular construction but certainly a barn is recorded as being on this site in 1639 and two were here in 1675. It would seem reasonable to assume therefore that this conversion could well be one of those.

Barn conversions are nothing new. Historically, barns and other buildings have regularly been turned into or used for housing and, perhaps less frequently though not unusually, houses have become barns. But in the past (a rather general term for a very big place) construction methods and building materials were not much different whether a building was to be agricultural, domestic or even ecclesiastical. Conversion and change of use was never that difficult and would almost always be easier and cheaper than building anew.

But then came the industrial revolution and all its resultant social and technological change. And in the twentieth century came further developments and an increasingly bewildering supply of new building materials and all their attendant regulations. These, combined with the post-second world war glut of redundant farm buildings supplied builders and architects, many of whom had little understanding of the harmonious relationship between landscape and materials, with an aesthetically dangerous programme of potential development. Some barns have survived the transition from one use to another and some have even been improved but these are very few. Most remain as pitiful and all too obvious reminders of the loss of our once instinctive bond with the land and with the rest of nature. Sadly, this is the result here, where even the thatch seems to have been put on with a ruler.

In *The Pattern of English Building* (1972) Alec Clifton-Taylor wrote that thatchers frequently become stylistically over-enthusiastic when working on dormers, gables and ridges and that an emphasis on fussy detailing is inevitably tiresome. He was right, as he so often was, and had the planning authority and the architect responsible for this conversion read and taken note of his opinions, the result could have been so much better. When, I wonder, will ordinary architects, planners and builders be educated in a school or discipline of aesthetics which is not rooted in the shallow inconsequentialities of Hollywood and Disney? When, in essence, will we be able to witness a return to the instinctive sensibilities of the artisans who built this once delightful barn all those years ago? One of the many answers is when we recognise that sophistication is about honesty and simplicity and purity. It is not, as so often seems the case, anything at all to do with cleverness or complexity. Another answer might be when those ordinary architects and builders are not hide-bound by reams of building regulations which might well be applicable to a development of new urban housing but which are often wholly inappropriate for a building which started its life several centuries ago.

This, I fear, will be a long time coming – and long enough for a great many more barn conversions as aesthetically displeasing and insulting as this.

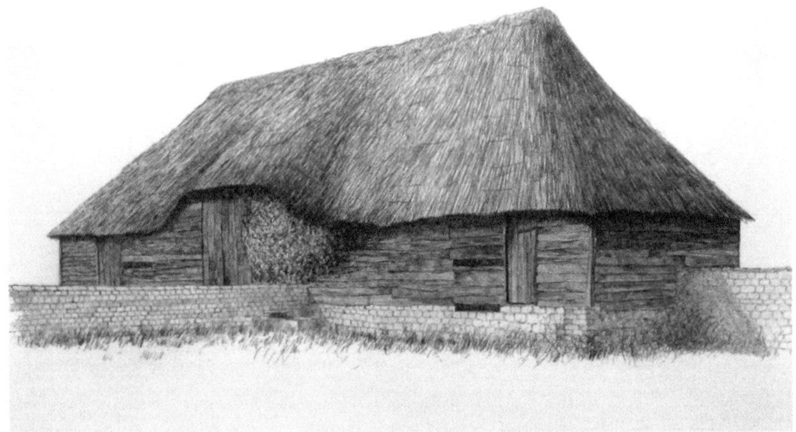

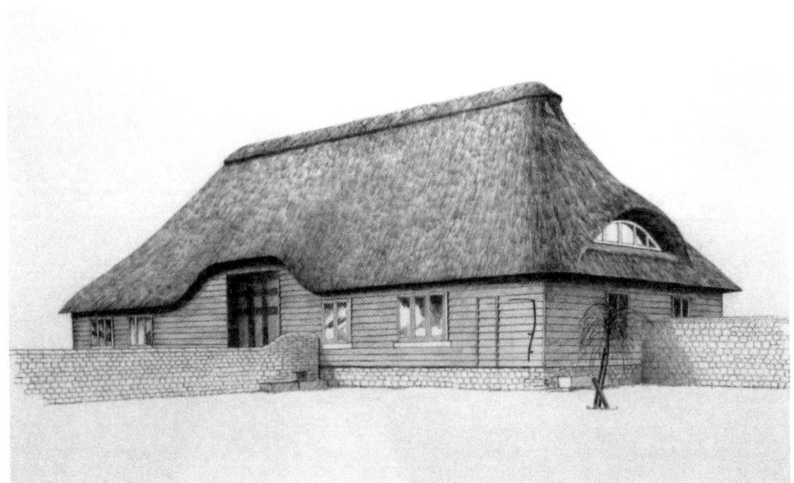

INDEX